There Is Joy In My Heart And Muck On My Shoe

KATHLEEN K WHITE

WESTBOW PRESS®
A DIVISION OF THOMAS NELSON
& ZONDERVAN

Copyright © 2022 Kathleen K White.

All rights reserved. No part of this book may be used or reproduced by any means, graphic, electronic, or mechanical, including photocopying, recording, taping or by any information storage retrieval system without the written permission of the author except in the case of brief quotations embodied in critical articles and reviews.

This book is a work of non-fiction. Unless otherwise noted, the author and the publisher make no explicit guarantees as to the accuracy of the information contained in this book and in some cases, names of people and places have been altered to protect their privacy.

WestBow Press books may be ordered through booksellers or by contacting:

WestBow Press
A Division of Thomas Nelson & Zondervan
1663 Liberty Drive
Bloomington, IN 47403
www.westbowpress.com
844-714-3454

Because of the dynamic nature of the Internet, any web addresses or links contained in this book may have changed since publication and may no longer be valid. The views expressed in this work are solely those of the author and do not necessarily reflect the views of the publisher, and the publisher hereby disclaims any responsibility for them.

Any people depicted in stock imagery provided by Getty Images are models, and such images are being used for illustrative purposes only.
Certain stock imagery © Getty Images.

ISBN: 978-1-6642-7447-1 (sc)
ISBN: 978-1-6642-7448-8 (hc)
ISBN: 978-1-6642-7446-4 (e)

Library of Congress Control Number: 2022914240

Print information available on the last page.

WestBow Press rev. date: 08/15/2022

Scripture quotations taken from The Holy Bible, New International Version® NIV® Copyright © 1973 1978 1984 2011 by Biblica, Inc. TM. Used by permission. All rights reserved worldwide.

Scripture quotations are from the ESV® Bible (The Holy Bible, English Standard Version®), copyright © 2001 by Crossway, a publishing ministry of Good News Publishers. Used by permission. All rights reserved.

Scripture taken from The Message. Copyright © 1993, 1994, 1995, 1996, 2000, 2001, 2002. Used by permission of NavPress Publishing Group.

Scripture taken from The Voice™. Copyright © 2012 by Ecclesia Bible Society. Used by permission. All rights reserved.

Scripture is taken from GOD'S WORD®, © 1995 God's Word to the Nations. Used by permission of Baker Publishing Group.

The Christian Standard Bible. Copyright © 2017 by Holman Bible Publishers. Used by permission. Christian Standard Bible®, and CSB® are federally registered trademarks of Holman Bible Publishers, all rights reserved.

Scripture taken from the New King James Version® Copyright © 1982 by Thomas Nelson. Used by permission. All rights reserved.

Scripture taken from the King James Version of the Bible.

Scripture taken from the New Century Version®. Copyright © 2005 by Thomas Nelson. Used by permission. All rights reserved.

Scripture quotations marked (NLT) are taken from the Holy Bible, New Living Translation, copyright ©1996, 2004, 2015 by Tyndale House Foundation. Used by permission of Tyndale House Publishers, a Division of Tyndale House Ministries, Carol Stream, Illinois 60188. All rights reserved.

Scripture quotations taken from the (NASB®) New American Standard Bible®, Copyright © 1960, 1971, 1977, 1995, 2020 by The Lockman Foundation. Used by permission. All rights reserved. www.lockman.org

Scripture quotations marked (LEB) are from the Lexham English Bible. Copyright 2012 Logos Bible Software. Lexham is a registered trademark of Logos Bible Software.

The Holy Bible, Berean Study Bible, BSB Copyright ©2016, 2018 by Bible Hub Used by Permission. All Rights Reserved Worldwide.

I dedicate *There Is Joy in My Heart and Muck on My Shoe* to my wonderful siblings, Kerry and Paul. I wrote this book as if I was with them. When we spend time together, we talk, laugh, work things out, and pray. Many times, we will be midsentence in a conversation and will transition to prayer. If you were privy to our time together, you wouldn't be able to tell when we were talking to God and when we were talking to each other. It just flows. God is a part of it.

Contents

Acknowledgments xiii
Introduction xv

Section 1: Prepare 1
Excuse Me, Dear, I Think You May Have Muck on Your Shoe 2
Prepare Ye 5
Full-On Trust 7
Thinketh 9
End of the Diving Board 11
I Ain't Scared of You! 13
Set a Plan in Your Heart 15
You Need a Hard Bottom and a Soft Heart 17
Fasting 19
Quack, Quack, Let It Roll off Your Back 21
Uptight Ninny 23
Been There, Done That—No More 25

Section 2: Shock 29
Take This Cup 30
More Than I Can Handle 32
Move Over, You're Blocking Me 34
Protection 36
Move Along 37

Section 3: Share 41
Settle 42
This Is Gossip, Not Prayer 44
Balm of Gilead 46
I Can See 49
Wisdom 51

Section 4: Grace 55
Adored 56
Details 58
Shine... 60
Laws to Love 63
Hurts 65
Not My Will, but Yours Be Done................................67
Pigs Don't Wear Pearls 69
Doing Right by You... 71
Purity Falling from Heaven.. 73

Section 5: Mourn..77
Hacked 78
I Don't Get It... 79
Bring Us Godly Sorrow..81
The One He Loves 82
Hug Them, Lord... 84
Ashes for Beauty 85

Section 6: Angry... 89
Why I Think We Have Cusswords 90
Vengeance... 92
Go Get 'Em 94
Robots versus Free Will.. 96
Casuistry Voices... 99
Blind or Seeing? 101
Huge Gap 104
Epiphany... 106
Let's Celebrate..108
Surrender 110
Faith 112
Hope.. 114
By Faith 116

Section 7: Rest 119
My Peter Pan Trip... 120
You Know What I'm Saying? No, No I Do Not!....................... 122
Deliberately Nailed 125

Real Heroes 127
Take It Personally 129
Honesty 131
One Good Decision Away 133

Section 8: Dump **137**
Licking Your Wounds 138
That Is Just Plain Nasty 140
Multitude of Sins 141
Teachable 143
Blessings and Judgment 145
Written in the Sand 147
The Thumb 149
Taking Out the Trash 151
Letting Go 153
Shots of Poison 155
Treats 157

Section 9: Forgiveness **161**
Sitting in the Dank Corner 162
Notice: Scapegoat Season Closed Permanently 164
Stones versus Flesh 166
Forgive Me! 169
My Bad 171
Forgive First 173
Grace Bombs 174

Section 10: Never Mind **177**
I. Don't. Care. 178
Rejoice! 180
Joke Night, because Even if Things Are Not Okay, It's Okay to Laugh—It's Healing! 182
Who 184
Pilate's Final Say 186
Brokenhearted but Full of Compassion 188
Doors Open 190
No Matter What 192
Before, Beside, Behind—Time Traveler 194

Fruit of the Spirit 196
What's Right with You 198
Overcomer 200
Take This Last Bite of Wisdom, Then You Tie Your Shoes and
Get Back Out There! 202

Section 11: Hurt Again 205
How Long? 206
Jump Back In 208
Relationships 210
Ask 212
The Bench 214
Healthy Fear 216
Love Always Protects 218
Sea Glass 220
Rough People 222

Section 12: Live Life 225
Hunter or the Hunted? 226
Backpack 228
Generous 230
Snort Laughter 232
Expired Party 234
Well-Liked 236
Sifting 238
"Live Well" Lifestyle 239
Water 240
I'm Hungry 241
This Little Light of Mine 243
Notecards 245
Sing, Shout, and Dance 247
Hey, Can You Play Today? 249
I'm Good 251
Getting Mileage out of Life 253
Farewell 255

Acknowledgments

A huge thank-you to my parents for encouraging me, for reading the manuscript countless times, and for their fun way of living life.

Thank you, Christy, for all your help with editing and with life!

I want to thank my sweet husband, Daniel, who is so kind about the time I spend with my parents and friends. He knows I am better for it.

Thank you to my family for encouraging me and giving me the time to write. Thank you to all the men in my life: Harrison, Philip, Andrew, and Daniel. Y'all keep it real and make me whole. I wouldn't want my life any other way. I love all of you.

Introduction

The Journey to Joy, Even if You Have Muck on Your Shoe

Life happens. Stepping in a mess happens! If you can have muck on your shoe and still maintain joy in your heart, then you are living! Sometimes the muck on your shoe is huge and life-changing; sometimes it is messy and stays messy. Muck sometimes represents irritating inconveniences. You go through different stages where you run into difficult times. You can be in shock, need grace, get angry, mourn, rest, need to be forgiven and forgive, and be in the dumps. Eventually you want to move on and have a great life. Life is a journey. It is the pain, the joy, and the relationship with God that makes life worth living. You are going to face hard times again and again as part of life. When you live on earth, you often step in muck. This should not define you. Earth is not our final destination, so clean up the muck and get on with the only life you will ever have.

If only it were that easy.

When you are hurting, sometimes you can barely get through the day. Daily devotions are easier to digest when you feel like a chewed-up mess. So, let's take one day at a time. Everything will be okay. Write, scribble, pray, and take your time with *There Is Joy in My Heart and Muck on My Shoe*. Please know that this book was born through my own deep pain, sin, selfishness, and sorrow, and is the result of my own journey. If by sharing my story helps you with your story, then we both win. Hard things happen to everyone. You will get through any hard time you are facing. You will be better than okay if you choose wisely. After a while, your pain could become a blessing.

This book of devotionals is divided into twelve sections: Prepare, Shock, Share, Grace, Mourn, Angry, Rest, Dump, Forgiveness, Never Mind, Hurt, and Living Life.

Section 1

PREPARE

Get ready, think, plan!
Enjoy the adventure of your only lifetime even
if it's not perfect, because it rarely is.

What exactly is muck? What does it stand for? For the purposes
of *There Is Joy in My Heart and Muck on My Shoe*, I describe
muck as things that happen that one is not expecting and
that aren't very much fun or are downright miserable.

It happens. Sometimes it is just a minor inconvenience; sometimes it is life-changing; sometimes you watch someone you love suffer. It's just part of life. It happens! Before you step in the muck, prepare for it, because the Lord knows there is a pile of mess around every corner. Life is a mixed-up batter of messy, hard, beautiful, fun, and sometimes serious muck. If right now you aren't in a gigantic pile of muck, then prepare yourself while you still have time. God did not say when you become a Christian that you should expect things to be perfect. He said the very opposite:

"I have told you these things, so that in Me you may
have peace. In this world you will have trouble. But take
heart! I have overcome the world" (John 16:33).
So, take heart, my friend, and prepare for the
messy parts of this wonderful life.

On the following pages you will find devotions to
help prepare you for stepping in a mess.

Excuse Me, Dear, I Think You May Have Muck on Your Shoe

> Mary treasured up all these things and pondered them in her heart.
> —Luke 2:19

Mary shows us how to really live. Mary has muck on her shoe and joy in her heart. My question for you to think about is, why is the modern-day Nativity scene so sanitized? If Mary, Joseph, and Jesus could see today's take on the Nativity scene, they probably wouldn't recognize it. Their thoughts: *What? Seriously? That's not right. Please add some more dirt, hay, manure, spiders, roaches, the mess from birth, and a lot more odor. Really? This is how you people portray it?*

The place was dirty, with spiderwebs everywhere, and bugs and manure had the run of the place. Excuse me, but it had no bed, no midwife, and absolutely no doctor, and it stank. There was excrement all over Mary's and Joseph's shoes! If we could just plop down into this scene and smell the odors, see all the animals, and feel the stress of the situation, we would not sanitize this picture. Mary's inexperience and Joseph's naivete (maybe that is why it's a Nativity—naive) are both very overwhelming. Please tell me that there was someone to help Mary deliver Jesus. Please tell me someone had mercy on them. These details are left out. Is it because that part just isn't pretty, or because there are some things we just shouldn't share?

Birth is messy—really messy, scary, and beautiful.

It's natural to look at the Nativity from our perspective. Mary had surely seen many babies being born and probably had helped deliver them. Maybe Joseph stepped outside, and Mary quietly had her baby and tended to all the details herself. Very impressive—no wonder there are so many statues of Mary! We are very spoiled nowadays!

Did Mary cry out or just silently have Jesus? How was the umbilical cord cut? Can you imagine having Mary describe the birth of Jesus at a baby shower? Wouldn't you like to sit down next to her and get all the details over some quiche and coffee?

Just when Joseph and Mary were getting Jesus comfy and adjusting to the smell and the animals, a miracle emerged. While they were busy cleaning up the manure and Jesus (What water did they use? Was it even boiled?), singing angels appeared to some shepherds in a lonely field. A huge bright star appeared over the stable. Dirty, frightened shepherds obeyed the announcement to come and see Jesus. Right there, with a little muck on Mary's and Joseph's feet, an entire host of angels came to worship and announce the good news.

When one angel shows up, the first thing that is typically said to us human folk is, "Do not fear." When a whole host of angels show up and start singing, silent holy awe overtakes you. The heavenly Father was presenting His human and holy Son as an infant to the world. This miracle was on full display. It was dirty, hard, humble, and miraculous! The Bible says, "Mary treasured up all these things and pondered them in her heart" (Luke 2:19). You know she did! She remembered the angel telling her she had been chosen to bring God's Son to earth. She remembered this amid the stench of the animals, the sight of her husband, the dirty shepherds, the tiny infant hands and feet, and the bright star illuminating it all. She was an authentic woman, one who had muck on her shoe and a song in her heart. She was a friend, a wife, and a mother, and someone I would love to meet.

So, if you have messy stuff on your shoe or in your life like Mary, Joseph, and I do, and if sometimes you don't smell or feel good, then you are living a full life.

We can learn to be like Mary with muck on our shoes and the song of Christ in our hearts as we thrive amid this wonderful thing called life. Life happens: the good, the bad, the tragic, the boring, the wonderful, and the miraculous all happen. Miracles are always in front of us, and most often we experience them among the hard things like Mary did. The stories of life can be funny, hard, and beautiful and, more often than not, full of glimpses of God's glory.

BYOB (Bible or beer—both work, as long as you don't use the Bible as a coaster for your beer) and enjoy this quirky, raw, real devotional book about life, struggle, how to handle hard times, and how much God loves each one of us.

REFLECTION

Do you think Mary had an easy time (being an unwed pregnant teenager) explaining this miracle to her fiancée and family?

How would you react if you were her parents, friend, or fiancée?

How can you be more vulnerable and real with others?

Are you able to have joy and praise the Lord even when you are having difficult times?

PRAYER

Lord, teach me to have a song of praise in my heart to You while I dwell on earth. Help me praise You and see Your goodness, even while there may be difficulties in my life. Help me, Lord, to have a joyful demeanor. I love You, God. Amen.

Prepare Ye

The beginning of the good news about Jesus the Messiah, the Son of God, as it is written in Isaiah the prophet: "I will send My messenger ahead of you, who will prepare your way, a voice of one calling in the wilderness, 'Prepare the way for the Lord, make straight paths for Him.'" And so, John the Baptist appeared in the wilderness, preaching a baptism of repentance for the forgiveness of sins. The whole Judean countryside and all the people of Jerusalem went out to him. Confessing their sins, he baptized them in the Jordan River. John wore clothing made of camel's hair, with a leather belt around his waist, and he ate locusts and wild honey. And this was his message: "After me comes the One more powerful than I, the straps of whose sandals I am not worthy to stoop down and untie. I baptize you with water, but He will baptize you with the Holy Spirit."
—Mark 1:1–8

Life here on earth is just like living out of a suitcase. Pack your suitcase prudently with wisdom, the fear of God, love, joy, peace, patience, kindness, faithfulness, self-control, faith, truth, forgiveness, laughter, the armor of God, and some grace bombs. Being prepared makes life so much better. When you prepare for what comes next or what might come next, life turns out much better.

We must prepare all the time. We are constantly preparing for the future: plans, goals, degrees, weddings, children, jobs, retirement, etc. God knew we needed to prepare for His Son. It is important to prepare for what comes next. It is wise; it makes life easier; and it helps with transitions. John the Baptist was the guy responsible for preparing the people for Jesus. His one and only focus was to get them ready for Jesus. Just like John, we should also prepare to be in the presence of Jesus.

At the very least, one could say that John the Baptist was one interesting dude. He was an oddity, even by today's standards. Eating wild locusts and honey as one's only meals is rad and destroys any fad diet around. Wearing camel's hair coats in the desert beats any episode of the *Man vs. Wild* show that I've ever seen. John just doesn't get through the desert to some safe place;

he thrives in the desert. What is great about John is that his heart was not about himself. His entire life's purpose was to prepare the people's hearts to be ready for Jesus. People came to John to repent, get baptized, and prepare their hearts for Jesus. People were so intrigued by John that they left their normal, tidy lives to see him in the wild desert.

In the wild, you get raw. You get real. Your heart gets right. You see the mighty stars and you know it's not all about you. Your heart is open. You prepare for God.

If you have never heard "Prepare Ye the Way of the Lord" by David Haskell, from *Godspell*, I recommend you listen to it. It is beautiful. It starts out as a whisper and then ends in a full crescendo. It is like starting off thanking the Lord, praising the Lord, and then, in tears, worshipping the Lord. Let this song take you on a journey to prepare you to be in the presence of God.

Lord, prepare our hearts.

REFLECTION

Do you enjoy being alone? When was the last time you looked at the stars at night or witnessed a sunrise or a sunset?

Describe what a date with Jesus would look like to you.

Why not go ahead and go out on a date with Him? Can you imagine what it would be like to date Jesus every day?

PRAYER

Lord, thank You for all Your blessings. Thank You for clean air, for forgiving me, and for Jesus dying on the cross for my sins. Lord, You are amazing and all-powerful. Nothing is impossible for You. I give You my praise. Lord, forgive me for being rude to You and not checking in on You. Help me be a good friend to You. You know my heart and concerns, and You can handle it all. I too want to know Your heart and concerns. How are You? How can I serve You? I love You. You are amazing. Help me to obey You and bring You honor. Amen.

Full-On Trust

> Those who know Your name trust in You, for You, Lord, have never forsaken those who seek You.
> —Psalm 9:10

We need to have full-on trust because when we really trust the Lord, we can handle life when we step in something awful or someone we love has something awful happen to them. When we live with our hearts and hands wide open to God and know that we are just passing through this spot on earth and that it is not our final destination, we have a peace that passes all understanding. Everything belongs to God, and we live like all belongs to God. This allows us to completely trust our heavenly Father, no matter what.

I have a dear friend named Hope who is an example of living as if everything belongs to God. Sometimes I am surprised she and I are friends. She is very glamorous, pretty, and put together. If my hair could look like hers for just twenty minutes, I would be thrilled. She is kind and a lover of God. She has a down-to-earth soul and is very classy at the same time. The following story is just one example of how Hope lives her life by completely trusting God: When her son Josh was around eight years old, he was playing hide-and-seek with his two older sisters, and he had an awful accident. Being a competitive boy, he climbed up to the top of the tree near the road to really hide from his twin sisters. The branch didn't hold him, and he fell and landed on the road on his head. A neighbor was on a walk and saw him passed out on the road with blood coming out of his head. The neighbor quickly ran to the door and alerted Hope and her husband.

Hope has a kind of faith that can move mountains. She had a rough childhood, but because she knows Jesus, she let Him turn this situation into something beautiful. She had already previously lost a child. On the way to the hospital, she told God, "Josh is Yours. He always has been. If You want to take him, take him." It makes me cry because of her beautiful total surrender to God and her awesome faith and trust. Hope's child Natalie was already in heaven. Maybe Hope's heart had already become softer and wiser, and she realized that her kids were never really hers, that they belonged to God. That is full-on trust.

Josh was not given a good prognosis at the hospital, but then he slowly began to heal, and eventually healed completely. He had no long-term effects from this awful accident except maybe some fantastic ones, such as realizing he had parents who know he belongs to God and that he was a son who knew he belonged to God. Josh is a wonderful young man. He loves the Lord and is an outstanding example to others. Lucky for him, the apple didn't fall far from the tree. Josh is a lot like his mom. He has a full-on trusting kind of faith.

The sooner we learn to live like Hope, the happier we will be. This is not our last destination. We can trust God. Let's live with full-on trust!

REFLECTION

Do you trust God no matter what—if your child dies, if you have cancer, if your spouse leaves you, if you go bankrupt?

Does your pain and heartache bring you closer to God, where you allow Him to comfort you, or does it make you angry and cause you to run from God?

PRAYER

Holy Father, let us trust You. Help us completely surrender to You. We don't know the future, but You do. "The Lord is good to all, and His tender mercies are over all His works" (Psalm 145:9). Your tender mercies sustain us. Give us Your peace that passes all understanding. All is Yours. If you take our loved ones, we will see them again in heaven. Your tender mercies sustain us! Hold us and our loved ones tight, Jesus. Help us to live for You. Remind us that earth is not our final destination. In Jesus's holy name. Amen.

Thinketh

> For as he thinketh in his heart, so is he.
> —Proverbs 23:7 (KJV)

We attract what we think. When we look for good, we find good. When we look for the bad, we find bad. Even when life is tough, if we are trained to think right, we'll get through the tough spot. Think smart and pure! Prepare a pure thought life. We humans have an amazing, mostly untapped ability to control our thoughts. It takes discipline and isn't always easy to control your thoughts, but it's so worth it. You can control what you think about!

When my brother was in college, he and his buddies were trying to clean up their act. They decided that if they said a dirty word, they would do twenty push-ups immediately, wherever they were. They did push-ups in the cafeteria, at a bar, at track practice, and even in the classroom. Then one day my brother just started doing push-ups without saying a bad word. When his friends asked him why, he said it was because he had just been thinking an ugly thought. I love that my brother knew it went much deeper than just what one says; it is what one thinks. The King James Version uses the best word to describe what is going on in one's soul and mind: *thinketh*.

What we think about, we become. Remember the Sunday school song, "O Be Careful, Little Eyes"? I'm going to add a new verse to it: "O be careful, little mind, what you think. O be careful, little mind, what you think. For the Father up above is looking down with love, so be careful, little mind, what you think."

REFLECTION

Read Philippians 4:8 and 2 Corinthians 10:5. Do you really believe that you can control what you think about? If so, how?

Do you believe God knows every secret of your heart and still loves you? Is that too good to be true? How do you respond if you believe He really does know every secret of your heart and still loves you?

PRAYER

God, You know we humans want to look good on the outside. In Psalm 44:21 it says You know the secrets of the heart. You know my secrets. You see all. You can create in me a clean heart! O God, You can renew a right spirit within me! Your sacrifice on the cross is not wasted. I am Yours. My sins are canceled on the cross. Take my thought life and especially take my secret thoughts. Father, bless me with being beautiful on the inside to You. Make me pure. Help me think about whatever is right, pure, lovely, admirable, excellent, and worthy of praise. Thank You for loving me. In Jesus's name. Amen.

End of the Diving Board

What do you know about tomorrow? How can you be so sure about your life? It is nothing more than a mist that appears for only a little while before it disappears.
—James 4:14 (CEV)

When we know this earth is not our final resting place, we live more intentionally. We aren't getting off the earth alive. We prepare for how we emotionally want to go out. Humans are amazing. We can control who we become. Each of us has an internal dial that decides what to concentrate on, what to remember, and what kind of people we want to be. Sometimes it takes some growing up to realize we have this dial inside of us and that we have more power over who we become than we originally thought. Hard things that happen can strengthen us or break us. That decision is up to us. We decide who we want to be.

One of the best "life dial" experiences I ever had was when I was working at a retirement home in my early twenties during the 1990s. I worked with the "greatest generation" and heard all their wonderful stories, sometimes the same ones about fifty times. It was mostly women, with a few good-looking roosters and only one actual pain in the derriere. Some of them were very beautiful on the inside and outside. Others were as mean and as ornery as a snake. They had all lived through World War II and had been young women and young moms during that time period. They lived with no communication for months from their husbands and other loved ones. Telegrams announced that their loved ones were gone. Some were strengthened, and some stayed surrounded by some terrible memories. It was interesting to be around so many people at the end of their diving boards of life when I was young and starting out. Wisdom was free for the taking, and these wonderful women shared! If you don't know what to fix for dinner, just start sautéing an onion in butter and the entire house will smell good, then it will look like you have a plan. Yum. Always cook with an iron pot. Ginger is good for you. These wonderful women reminded me often that the Velveteen Rabbit was right: you will get loose in the joints and become very shabby, but you will also become real. The one thing that I really took away from that experience was the idea that who we are today gets magnified as we get older. What do we want to magnify—terrible memories, being jilted, or a living life well and being full of faith, forgiveness, laughter, and love? Decide now, because the end of the diving board is really not that far away.

You oversee who you are, and you are in charge of who you become. You are not just floating along like a feather in the wind, as Forrest Gump wonders. He is the perfect example of being in charge of who you become.

REFLECTION

What kind of older person do you want to be?

What would you like said about you at your funeral?

How can you become the person God created you to be?

Are you prepared for death?

PRAYER

God, You know life is short. Give me a spirit of excellence. Let me radiate Your love to others every day. Set in my heart Your course. Take away anything in me that does not bring You glory. Get rid of all bitterness in me. Allow what life brings my way to make me better and never bitter. In Psalm 40:2 it says You lifted me out of the slimy pit, out of the mud and mire; You set my feet on a rock and gave me a firm place to stand. Lord, I don't want to get to the end of my days with mire and muck all over me. I am Yours. I ask You to make me beautiful on the inside and out. Because You give me a firm place to stand, I will stand. I will stand and trust in You. Lord, I ask You to pour out the blessings of trust, beauty, love, protection, and faith on me for all the days of my life. Let me celebrate the good, forgive others, learn from the hard, and become who You created me to be. Amen.

I Ain't Scared of You!

> Peace I leave with you; My peace I give you. I do not give as the world gives. Do not let your hearts be troubled and do not be afraid.
> —John 14:27

Sometimes we need not step in a pile to act like a piece of muck. Sometimes we get so anxious and worried about the pile of pain around the corner that we live as if there is mire all over us because we know there might be someday.

Oh my goodness, grow up and clean out your thoughts! Train and prepare your thought life; don't rob yourself by dwelling on what might happen. I am so tired of worrying and being afraid of what might happen. I have an active imagination and I can come up with some scary scenarios. This is not healthy, and I'm done! Join me! Let's shake off this lie forever!

What we fear the most is what we pray about and obsess over the most! Car wrecks, cancer, accidents, an unfaithful spouse, a child dying, losing a job, falling into financial ruin, never meeting a person to marry, being lonely.... We keep tripping over what we think about. It's as if we invite our fears for dinner, have a glass of wine with them, and then ask them to stay for dessert and sometimes even a nightcap! Why? Let's go face-to-face with that fear and the terrible place we imagine in our nightmares and then kick these out of our house forever. Go ahead. Imagine the worst thing. Dwell on it. Allow it to happen in your mind. Then ask yourself: "Will you make it through it? Will God be there for me? Will I be strong enough? What if it happens?" I think the answer is that God will be there for you. Will it be fun? Probably not. Will you grow tremendously? Yes. Will you become better or bitter? Choose now that no matter what happens, you will allow God to make you better. Decide that no matter what happens, you will let it make you more relatable, kinder, and more empathetic. I used to tell my kids when they had an overly worried attitude that the worst thing that could happen is that they would die, but that was actually the best thing because they would be in heaven with God. So, what do you really have to worry about? Give it up. Give it to God. Kick it out of your mind. Stop letting it rob you of joy and of life. Release its hold on you. Unshackle yourself. Kick those lies and the life robber, the devil, out of your house forever. Don't act as if you have junk all over you just because you might at some point.

Train your mind. Sometimes I just keep repeating Philippians 4:8 in my mind: "Finally, brothers and sisters, whatever is true, whatever is noble, whatever is right, whatever is pure, whatever is lovely, whatever is admirable—if anything is excellent or praiseworthy—think about such things." Literally go through that verse. Invite what is true, noble, right, pure, lovely, excellent, or praiseworthy, not just for dinner and a nightcap, but to be with you always. List it, pray for it, be grateful for it, and enjoy it. No more life robbers for you! Ain't nobody got time for that!

REFLECTION

How is fear your worst enemy? How does fear and worry rob you?

Read Ephesians 5:8-14 What can you do to stop being robbed by this life robber, fear?

PRAYER

God, forgive me for worrying about things that haven't happened. Forgive me, Lord, for letting worry and fear rob me of Your joy and being in the precious moment of now. God, in Jesus's name, take away the lies of fear and worry from me and my loved ones. I don't know what tomorrow holds, but I know You hold my tomorrow. No matter what happens, You will be there for me. God, it says in 2 Corinthians 10:5, "We demolish arguments and every pretension that sets itself up against the knowledge of God, and we take captive every thought to make it obedient to Christ." God, I ask that You demolish every argument and pretension that sets itself up against You. Take my thoughts captive and make them obedient to You. In 1 Corinthians 2:16, it says we have the mind of Christ. Thank You for giving me the mind of Christ. I am at peace, and I trust You. Amen.

Set a Plan in Your Heart

> David said to God, "I am in deep distress. Let us fall into the hands of the Lord, for His mercy is great; but do not let me fall into human hands."
> —2 Samuel 24:14

Okay, we will not live as if bad things are about to happen; we are going to be ready, smart, and prepared like a good army. We are ready and we know what to do, just in case. Dial in wise living mode! Thinking and predetermining how to react in every hard circumstance in life is a great idea. To be prepared in our hearts and minds for what life might bring is wise. Plan to fall into the hands of the Lord, not into the ways of humankind!

So far, I think I have lived in such a way that I try not to think about all the bad things that might happen and just avoid dwelling on these possibilities. It is like not preparing for retirement. We all need a detailed plan to pull out of our "What in the World Do I Do Now?" file. Wouldn't it be wise to be prepared to handle any situation? Why don't we teach such skills in school? My best advice for anyone is to go down some tragic dark roads in your mind, considering any unthinkably poor decisions. Think about how God would want you to respond to those situations. Please pray for God's protection from those dark and tragic parts of life, but also be prepared. Any good military has a plan for the what-ifs, the uh-ohs, and the shockers. Why should we be any different? Predetermine your reactions and make your plans. Maybe even act out your reactions in front of a mirror. I could make a board game featuring awful situations for us to practice reacting to. The winner would be the one with the highest number of calm and loving reactions! I really wish I had played that game before some shockers in my life banged down my door. If I had not been so self-righteous, I would have realized that I, as we all do, sin and fall to temptation. When the worst happens, don't allow yourself to be blindsided and react out of your fear, shame, hurt, shock, anger, immaturity, disappointment, and hormone-based emotions, along with reactions to your past. You can't undo critical reactions. God can, however, heal any situation and bring good out of anything. His mercy is never-ending.

We are each completely in charge of our own reactions. We can't control what happens to us or to our loved ones, but we can control how we ourselves react. Let's have a prepared life reaction plan. Let's know how God would want us to react. Let's practice how God wants us to react, and then let's react how He wants us to.

REFLECTION

Think about every scenario that could happen in life. List the good, the bad, and the awful.

Now set a plan in your heart for how God would want you to represent Him in each of these situations.

PRAYER

Lord, set my heart on You. You are in charge. You are my reactions. When I react, let it be You who reacts through me. Lord, cover me in Your mighty love, wisdom, and kindness. Protect me and others from human sinful reactions. Lord, go before me, beside me, and behind me. You are in charge. Amen.

You Need a Hard Bottom and a Soft Heart

> For God did not give us a spirit of timidity, but a spirit of power, of love, and of self-discipline.
> —2 Timothy 1:7

Having a heart bottom and a soft heart is important. No one wants to raise a bully or a wimp. A bully has a heart hard, doesn't forgive, and is mean to those around him. A wimp's heart is also hard, but the wimp cowers and lets people walk all over him. There is a precious balance of wisdom that needs to be attained. You want to be both strong (i.e., have a hard bottom) and kind (i.e., have a soft heart).

"Have a hard bottom and a soft heart" is what I would tell my kids often when they were growing up. What does that mean? After a while, they could answer that question. "Hard bottom" means you belong to God and therefore you are tough; you don't whine, manipulate, or cry to get attention; and you don't get offended easily. You know life can be tough, but you are tough too. "Soft heart" means you belong to God and therefore you are kind and personable; you see others in need and you help them; you forgive easily; and you are fun to be around. Life doesn't center on you. We would often talk about how it is ill-advised to have a soft bottom and a hard heart. That would be a disaster. A soft bottom means people walk all over you and basically you are a big baby. A hard heart means you let meanness get a hold of you and you become defensive, self-focused, and probably a manipulative bully. Be wise and stay aware to keep a hard bottom and a soft heart. Forgive, pray, read your Bible, and be ready for what comes.

Both a hard bottom and a soft heart get you through elementary school, middle school, high school, and life. Hard bottoms and soft hearts are necessary in the world we live in.

REFLECTION

Do you get offended easily? If so, how can you toughen up?

Are you quick to forgive?

Read Acts 4:29 How can you be both kind and strong?

PRAYER

Lord, thank You that through You I don't have a spirit of timidity, but a spirit of power, of love, and of self-discipline. Keep me aware and help me have a hard bottom and a soft heart. Amen.

Fasting

So, He said to them, "This kind can come out by nothing, but prayer and fasting."
—Mark 9:29 (NKJV)

Fasting should be part of your life. A lifestyle of honoring God and realizing He is more important than anything else prepares your heart for what may come. God is God, and you are not. This is what fasting is all about: perspective! I think there are many types of fast. There are fasts that enable you to just feel the presence of God, fasts that you do to request something, fasts that cause you to discern, and fasts whose purpose is to pray for evil to be demolished.

Many times, the only way I know of to pray about a situation is through fasting. Sometimes it is a complete fast; sometimes I give up certain foods. But whatever type of fast it is, it causes me to pray differently. It is an earnest, doesn't-go-away kind of prayer, a full down-on-my-knees-or-face sort of prayer. It is the kind of prayer that I know only God can answer. Only miracles will work. Sometimes the miracle involves a change in my perspective, and sometimes it is a miracle that only God can do. He gets the credit. I just feel this peace that passes all understanding. It reminds me that God is in charge and that He's got me, the situation, and/or the person in His hands. When I give up something so little to concentrate on God's goodness and mercy, I get so much more peace and much more of a relationship with God than I ever thought possible. God is God, and I am not.

Fasting is powerful. Sometimes there are just circumstances that call for prayer fasting. Jesus knew that and explained it to us. At the end of the fast, you have peace. You are all prayed up. You know God has it under His control.

REFLECTION

What is something that you could give up in order to feel God's presence more acutely in your life?

Do you need to fast?

PRAYER

Lord, thank You for the beautiful peace that passes understanding that You give me. Thank You that I can be in Your presence. Thank You for hearing me. Thank You for prayer. I love You. Amen.

Quack, Quack, Let It Roll off Your Back

> You prepare a table before me in the presence of my enemies.
> You anoint my head with oil, my cup overflows.
> —Psalm 23:5 (ESV)

God can anoint us with oil. We can live slick! Oil up, baby! With the anointing of God, we can be prepared for anything! Since I didn't grow up in biblical times, it took me some living to understand what "anoint my head with oil" meant. Ducks have helped me understand this. Let me explain.

Ducks have a wonderful protective covering. It is the oils they get from their noses that protect them. When they groom themselves, they put on a protective covering of oil that covers their entire bodies. Baby ducklings don't have this oil until they mature. The mama duck grooms the baby ducklings with her nose, and that is how they get this protective oil. That is why baby ducklings can swim with their moms. Ducklings that get separated from their moms can't swim until they produce their own oils. They freeze to death. The water soaks right into their skin.

Nature teaches us many things. We need a protective covering, too. We need the oil of the Lord to protect us. We need to be like ducks. When things and people hurt us, we need to quack, quack, quack and let it roll off our backs. Wouldn't it be fun to just start quacking when you get your feelings hurt? Let's do it! Can't you just see your family looking at you as if you have lost your mind? *Quack, quack, quack.* Letting things roll off your back takes grooming. You need to groom your mind and heart to forgive yourself and others, not to be offended, and to think about whatever is true, honorable, just, pure, lovely, commendable, and worthy of praise. Groom your prayers to pray for others, and repeat often, "Father, forgive them for they know not what they do." Groom yourself not to be oversensitive, and pray that you won't easily take offense. Groom yourself to forgive others before they hurt you. Groom yourself to see the good and not the bad, to be positive, and to be a blessing to others. Groom your whole heart, mind, and soul to praise the Lord and be thankful. Groom yourself and ask the Holy Spirit to give you the anointing oil of beauty and forgiveness so you can quack, quack, quack and let it roll off your back.

Do you know what happens when God anoints you with oil? Your cup overflows. What a great way to live!

REFLECTION

Have you ever studied what it means to anoint with oil? Grab your Bible and find out! Read Exodus 30:32-33, Mark 6:13, James 5:14-15, Isaiah 61:1 and Luke 4:18

How can you live anointed?

PRAYER

Lord, in Psalm 23:5 it says, "You prepare a table before me in the presence of my enemies. You anoint my head with oil, my cup overflows." Lord, thank You for the table You prepared for me while I am in enemy territory. Lord, thank You for anointing me with Your oil that protects me and covers me in You. Because of Your love, my life overflows with kindness, forgiveness, and love. Amen.

Uptight Ninny

> Therefore, I tell you, her many sins have been forgiven—as her great love has shown. But whoever has been forgiven little loves little.
> —Luke 7:47

A ninny is someone who is uptight and thinks that he or she is untouchable in certain areas. Ninnies are self-righteous and judge the rest of the world. They are completely unaware that they do this. If you ask a ninny, they will tell you they are kind and loving, but they tend to be kind and loving only when others are kind and loving. Whatever you do, don't be an uptight ninny. Because I was an uptight ninny and must repent of having been a ninny in certain situations, I say this for anyone who might be a little ninnyish. If you can get all ninny off of you, you will be prepared to truly love others. You will be able to love the sinner, not the sin.

It's not fun getting the ick of ninnyish off you. If you have ever been knocked off your high horse as I have, then you know what I'm talking about. If it is my own personal sin, I convict myself, give myself a good flogging. Oh, but if it is one of my kids, Lord help them. I find myself punishing them as it were my only mission on earth.

Why would I "flog" myself or others? It is not my job to do so if I truly know Jesus. The problem is that I was covered in pristine, arrogant righteousness. This attitude told me that we humans don't deserve to be forgiven and we Christians, of all people, don't mess up! We must punish ourselves and live in misery. Haughty righteous arrogance that believes I had earned my right to be forgiven and blessed in the first place became the very air I breathed. I choked on my own convictions and threw up meanness. After much meanness and pain, I eventually learned to love and depend on Jesus like the very air I breathe. I now know God in a way I never thought possible. This blessing came through the hardships. My core screams out that all of life is from God. No one, especially me, deserves salvation, blessings, healing, miracles, mercy, and grace. It is an entirely free gift. I am very grateful for what I went through. I like myself so much better now.

God takes our broken repentant souls and wraps us in blankets of holy knowledge, peace that passes all understanding, and joy that comes from a right relationship with God

REFLECTION

Do you have any ninny attitudes? List them.

How would you define a ninny?

Who have you flogged?

Have you been flogged by yourself or others?

Do you fully realize how many sins God canceled for you?

Can you forgive yourself and others and be set free? How?

When you truly mess up, you don't have to pretend that you are good. This is very freeing. You have no expectations of a fake persona to fill. You can just be a forgiven, grateful, and humble person.

PRAYER

Lord, I lie flat on my face, praising You for Your salvation, blessings, healing, miracles, mercy, and grace. O Lord, my many sins have been forgiven. Lord, prepare our hearts to love others the way You love them. Prepare us to surround our situations in mercy, grace, and love. Teach us how to react to what live brings us. In Jesus's name. Amen.

Been There, Done That—No More

> Then Noah began farming and planted a vineyard. He drank of the wine and became drunk and uncovered himself inside his tent. Ham, the father of Canaan, saw the nakedness of his father, and told his two brothers outside. But Shem and Japheth took a garment and laid it upon both their shoulders and walked backward and covered the nakedness of their father; and their faces were turned away, so that they did not see their father's nakedness. When Noah awoke from his wine, he knew what his youngest son had done to him.
> —Genesis 9:20–24 (NASB)

I am begging you not to have any ninny in you whatsoever. It is the ugliest kind of sin; believe me, I experienced it. If there is one area of my life and one relationship that I could change, it would be how I treated someone who felt shame. I sometimes treat strangers better than I treat my family. My family wasn't supposed to experience shame. If you asked me, I was most certainly not a ninny. But I was, and because I was a ninny, I pretended to be a princess in a castle where the actual world didn't come knocking. If I had only known how to respond to shame, I would not feel so much shame now for how I treated my loved one. Please never be a ninny to others. If you are human, you sometimes succumb to making bad choices. How we treat others when they mess up depends on how much we know the love, mercy, and grace of God. We hope and pray that when we mess up, people will treat us how Christ would treat us.

We all have a little of Noah, Ham, Shem, and Japheth in us. Noah is described in the Bible as a righteous man. Even righteous men can make mistakes. He got ugly drunk. He is human. All of us mess up. Ham took advantage of this situation and dishonored his father by approaching him in his nakedness. Shem and Japheth honored their father and walked in backward with their faces turned away to cover him up. Noah, righteous, messed up; Ham took advantage; Shem and Japheth honored Noah and covered up his embarrassment. In college, I had a terrible experience with tequila and literally blacked out. I am very thankful I was with some Shem and Japheth people who took care of me. I don't even want to think about what could have happened otherwise. No Ham was there to dishonor me. I have been Shem and Japheth and have helped my friends in unpleasant situations. None of us want to be in Noah's shoes and cross the line of drinking from being buzzed to "I am not sure what happened." The latter is ugly, shameful, and embarrassing. Shem and Japheth were older and obviously deeply respected Noah. They knew that Noah was a good soul who drank too much and found himself in a bad place. They were very respectful and showed him much honor by walking in backward with a blanket and turning their faces from their father's nakedness. This story really is about much more than just drinking. It is about how we treat others in their shame.

I pray for you and me that not only may we have Shem and Japheth type of people in our lives, but also that we behave like Shem and Japheth toward others. May we walk in backward in our relationships with others in their shame and embarrassment with our faces turned away and cover them with grace, mercy, and love.

REFLECTION

Why do you think this story is in the Bible?

How do you handle mess-ups, embarrassment, and shame?

Is there any area in your life where tight religious rules, combined with layers of expectations, prejudices, or your past behavior, prevent you from loving others or responding as Christ would?

PRAYER

Lord, forgive me. Forgive me for when I haven't walked in backward in my relationships, with my head turned, and covering up and giving mercy to others in shame. Teach me to love like You love, to forgive like You forgive, and to give mercy and grace to others. God, where I have shamed others, cancel its authority, and hug and heal those I have hurt. God, never allow me to make others feel shame again. Protect me from bad choices, and let me love and care for Your children no matter what. Amen.

CONCLUSION OF SECTION I

Section I: Prepare is summed up by the sweet life-giving verses in James 2:12–13:

"Speak and act as those who are going to be judged by the law that gives freedom, because judgment without mercy will be shown to anyone who has not been merciful."

Mercy triumphs over judgment!

Let God cover you and your life in mercy!

Section II

SHOCK

You just stepped in it! It happens! You are in shock.

You were thinking about what pillows would look nice on your couch, what your dinner plans were, and when you should exercise today. Normal thoughts, normal life. Then you stepped in some mess, either your own or that of someone you love, or just the mess that life brings. Cancer diagnoses, accidents, a death, an awful choice, a sin exposed, a financial disaster, a market crash, betrayal, or just an ordinary mess. All are tough. Life is tough. Life is full of challenges, and involves refining, wiping up after the mess, and learning from it. We all step in tough times. It is part of the wonderful adventure called life.

When we step in it deep, we wish we hadn't.
That's all we can think about at first:

Make it go away!

On the following pages you will find devotions
to help you when you are in shock.

Take This Cup

Father, if You are willing take this cup from Me: yet not My will, but Yours be done.
—Luke 22:42

When I am in shock, I pray this prayer repeatedly: "Lord, take this cup from me. Take it. Take it. Take it!" The second part, I whisper, knowing that God knows what is best. He does. I submit. I say, "Get me there, God. Help me say and mean, 'Not my will, but Yours be done.'" Jesus prayed this prayer too. When Jesus made this request, He knew what He was about to succumb to. He knew the future. He knew what the next couple of days would entail. I like the humanity of this request because I can relate to the begging quality of "Make this go away!"

Just as Jesus did, be real and pray and ask for this cup to be taken away. Pray in your own words mixed with His:

"If You are willing, because I know You can, take this cup from me: it is awful, full of shame, separation, desperation, judgment, pain, misunderstanding, rejection, loneliness, agony, death, and evil. Yet not my will, but Yours be done. I submit. If it is necessary, let Your will be done. God, even Jesus needed angels. So do I. Let Your angels appear and strengthen me."

And what Jesus was about to face wasn't easy. It was horrific. It was the worst of the worst. Jesus, they mocked You, crowned You with a crown of thorns, and flogged You almost to death, and You were rejected by Your best friends. You heard one of Your best friends swear and say three times that he didn't know You. Those who were in positions of religious authority, those who were supposed to know God, framed You! Misunderstanding, judgment, and sheer cruelty by these leaders in positions of authority tossed You back and forth. You got mocked some more and were spit on; another guilty man was set free, leaving You to die. You were innocent, but You didn't defend yourself. You did not get rescued by God or by those who loved You. You barely hung onto life, nailed to a cross, the most humiliating death one could endure. The crowd made fun of You! One of the very men who hung next to You cursed at You. Yet, You still gave mercy to one criminal who asked at the very last minute for grace and to be let into Your kingdom. You had to watch

Your mother weep and see her heart break. You witnessed Your clothes being divided. The centurions gave You vinegar to drink when You were thirsty. You experienced ultimate darkness and separation from God with all the world's sins upon You. Finally, Your last desperate agonized words rang out for all eternity, "It is finished" (John 19:30).

If you have ever been desperate enough to ask God to take away something that you saw as awful, then you understand. More importantly, He understands.

REFLECTION

Since Jesus was both God and human, He asked not to have to go through with His crucifixion. Have you ever asked God to "take away this cup" and then also submitted to "not my will, but Yours be done"?

PRAYER

O Lord, sometimes we just don't want to go through what we see as awful. We can see pain, heartbreak, judgments, persecutions, and misunderstandings in our future. We ask You, Lord, just like Jesus, to take this cup of shame, sadness, hardness, and suffering away from us. We know You can. We also know that You care more about who we are than what we have to go through. So, Lord, through my tears, I claim not my will, but Yours be done. Amen.

More Than I Can Handle

> I have said these things to you, that in Me you may have peace. In the world you will have tribulation. But take heart; I have overcome the world.
> —John 16:33 (ESV)

Okay, so you still have the cup in front of you. It's not gone, and tears fall from your eyes. Your soul cries out: *I can't do this! This is more than I can handle!* I really don't like the statement "God never gives us more than we can handle." Who made that up, some pious person who lives in a castle? Of course, God gives us more than we can handle because He can handle it for us. I am taking that ceramic representation of a fairy tale saying that life is perfect, neat, and tidy and throwing it against cement reality. As the image crumbles, actual life emerges.

Sometimes you are in a place in life that you just can't handle. You feel broken. You just miscarried again, your husband just passed away, you didn't get into your dream school, you got used, mean and ugly things happened, you were betrayed, you were robbed, you were raped, you were fired, you got cancer, both your kids died in a car accident, you got left out again, you were talked about, you were misrepresented, you lost everything, you became deeply depressed, you were lonely, you were hungry, death took your loved one, you were homeless, and life was foul. This is where it is just too much! Not fair! Not at all fairy tale like! Too much, I tell you, too much! Grief, sin, and life were so heavy that you felt you were being crushed. You were flat on the floor, miserable, with earth's sins pinning you down. Every cell in your body screamed, "I can't handle it!"

The presence of God and the peace that passes all understanding sits down with each of us on the floor letting us know: *yes, this is too much for you, I'll handle this for you. Let it go.* And a soft verse is whispered: "Take heart, I have overcome the world" (John 16:33 ESV). God's got us. He can handle it.

REFLECTION

Do you subscribe to the belief that God never gives us more than we can handle?

Do you really believe that?

PRAYER

God, I need You to pick me up off the floor and hug me and hug those who are hurting. Life is too overwhelming right now, and I can't do it, but You can. You are not just my help, but You are my all. I just don't depend on You, I need You for every breath I breathe. I claim Galatians 2:20 for myself: "I am crucified with Christ, and it is no longer I that live, but Christ living in me." That life which I now live in the flesh, I live by faith in the Son of God, who loved me and gave Himself up for me. This is the only way I am going to get through this, Lord—and we both know it. Take over, always, in every breath I breathe. I can't do this, but You can. Thank You, God. Amen.

Move Over, You're Blocking Me

> Then they cried to the Lord in their trouble, and He delivered them from their distress.
> —Psalm 107:28

If you are talking to God and listening, then you know He has this situation you are in. You need not take over. Prayer goes places you can't. God hears you. Pray. Pray scripture. Pray earnestly.

Being a parent of adult children can be hard. There is a fine line between knowing when to talk or help and when to let them figure things out on their own. So, I resort to the knowledge that I can talk to God about my children, and God can talk to them. He is the Great Mediator.

"If you keep rescuing your children, then I can't." This is the still small voice I heard in my heart from God. I love my kids. I have been a stay-at-home mom for the past twenty-four years. When they hurt, I hurt. If they are happy, I celebrate. I fast and pray for them constantly. This whole parent–adult child relationship can be confusing and quite hairy and scary to navigate. I really don't know when to call, what to say, or if to say something or be quiet. During the most recent hard struggle with one of my kids, I knew I was told in that sweet small voice to let my child and God handle the messy situation. As in: no rescue from me. They need to grow up, become adults. Adults. On their own. Emotionally, physically, spiritually, all of it.

It is during trying times that I talk to God about my adult children. I talk to the Mighty Mediator, asking that His will be done. I pray God's promises over my children.

REFLECTION

Do you trust God enough to pray scripture and rest in the fact that He loves your children more than you do?

PRAYER:

Lord, let my children cry out to You in their trouble, and deliver them from their distress. As for me and my house, we will serve the Lord. Give them Your divine wisdom and direction. You who began a good work in them will complete it. You turn their hearts toward God. You give them divine protection, wisdom, success, and favor. Let them be as wise as serpents and as innocent as doves. They have the mind of Christ. Your plans are to bless them and prosper them and give them hope and a future. Let them have good friends and be good friends. Jesus, bind the fruit of the Spirit on them: love, joy, peace, patience, kindness, gentleness, faithfulness, and self-control. Let them think about whatever is good, true, pure, excellent, and worthy of praise. Give them Your mercy and grace. Let them love You with all their hearts, minds, and souls. Bless them, Lord. Favor them, Lord. Hug them, Lord. Let them be everything You created them to be. Let them walk in their anointing. Cover them in the blood of Jesus. Go before them, beside them, and behind them. Let them hear the words "Well done, good and faithful servant." Let Your will be their will and their will be Your will. Let them bring You glory. Lord, they are Yours. Rescue them. Bless them. I am getting out of the way. They need to depend on You to rescue, love, and bless them. I am giving them to You. They are adults. It is between You and them. I will pray for them but no longer block Your rescue efforts. In Jesus's name. Amen!

Protection

> But the Lord is faithful, and He will strengthen you and protect you from the evil one.
> —2 Thessalonians 3:3

I've got muck all over my life, and I need You, God, to protect me. I can't do this without Your holy protection.

The Lord does protect. It can be windy at the beach, especially in the afternoon. One day I and my family were at a beach that was enclosed by a rock barrier, and in the rock barrier there were absolutely no waves. The waves came right up to it but couldn't go past it. It was calm and swimmable. The water was like glass, but only in this area. God whispered to me in my heart that this is what He does for us when we ask for His hedge of protection. He surrounds us and gives us a peace that passes all understanding. There is calmness, beauty, and love in the middle of rough waves.

Let God protect you and hold you in His mighty arms.

REFLECTION

Do you believe that God can protect you even when you feel as if you are in Hades?

PRAYER

Lord, in Psalm 139:5 it says, You hem me in, behind and before, and You lay Your hand upon me." Thank You, God. I rest in Your protection. Amen.

Move Along

> Even though I walk through the darkest valley, I will fear no evil, for You are with me; Your rod and Your staff, they comfort me.
> —Psalm 23:4

When life is hard, the very worst thing you can do is to stay in that which is hard. Don't sit down in the hard and let it swallow you. Don't worship the problem, the pain, and the hurt. Don't replay the pain in your mind over and over again. Don't let it become the very air you breathe. Get the pain off replay.

Keep on moving. Don't sit down and have a picnic. I am not sure you should even stop to tie your shoe or blow your nose. Sometimes you just must get through the hard time with your head down and by walking at a quick pace. Keeping your head down and "flat moving it" can be a good thing. When you run uphill, the best advice I can give you is to keep your head down and look at the ground in front of you. Before you know it, you are at the top. When you run cross-country, running hills is part of the program. If you look at your feet, it is not as hard. If you look up and see how much farther you have to go, it can be quite discouraging.

Nothing lasts forever. Life is like a wave. Life is constantly changing and moving: it can be calm, you can be at the bottom, or at the crest, or surfing, or getting pulled out in an undertow, or crashing onto the shore. The more you live, the better you get at handling the waves and knowing nothing lasts forever. You don't stay in that which is bad or that which is perfect forever. Enjoy the ride.

The challenge is to intentionally make life as enjoyable as possible, but when it gets awful, do not, whatever you do, sit down in misery and stay there. Keep moving. There is no mention of sitting down or staying in Hades in Psalm 23:4. Keep moving. Fear no evil, because God is with you. His rod beats the enemy. His staff grabs you when you are about to trip or fall. You are protected and comforted wherever you go by the Good Shepherd.

REFLECTION

Nothing last forever. How are you doing with surfing life's waves?

PRAYER

Lord, teach me Your ways. Show me Your paths. You never said life would be easy. You did say that when, not if, but when I walk through the darkest valley, I will fear no evil, for You will be with me. Your rod and staff will comfort me. Lord, get me through the darkest valleys quickly and safely. Don't let me ever sit down and stay in these dark and evil places. Thank You for Your hedge of protection. Thank You that even in the season of darkness, You get me through it! In Jesus's name. Amen.

CONCLUSION OF SECTION II

Being in shock is hard.
Allow God to comfort you and hold you in His mighty arms.
Let God rock you like a baby.
I pray that you will feel the love and comfort of the Lord
and that you will fall asleep tonight in the arms of Jesus.

Section III

SHARE

To share or not to share?

You are looking around your pit of despair; you are perhaps starting to talk about your pile of difficulty, and you need to be careful. You need to decide whom to talk to, whom to tell, and how to handle your life now. Once you tell, people can't unhear, can't forget, and sometimes can't keep their mouths shut. You can't take it back.

Make me wise, Lord. Teach me Your ways.

On the following pages you will find devotions to help you decide if you should share, whom to share with, and whom to trust.

Settle

> Do not conform to the pattern of this world, but be transformed by the renewing of your mind. Then you will be able to test and approve what God's perfect will is—His good, pleasing, and perfect will.
> —Romans 12:2

Before you decide anything, let the matter settle. When life gets hard, it can be messy—hard-to-see-through messy. It is wise just to let things settle before you react or decide what to do next.

I live near the Chattahoochee River in Georgia. At times it can be beautiful and clear and you can see the rainbow trout's festive colors shining through the clear water, but when it rains, it gets muddy—red clay and chocolate muddy. This happens in life sometimes. A storm comes and we can't see clearly. Everything just gets muddled, confused, and difficult, and we can't think or see clearly. The river can take up to three days to clear and get back to normal. It is just a time thing. You just wait.

In life, sometimes things just need to settle, clear up. It is just a time thing. Allow problems and situations to settle. Sometimes the more you go stomping through the problems, the messier it gets. Just like the river. Let it clear up. Then you can see clearly.

REFLECTION

Is it hard for you to let things settle?

When in the past do you wish you had given a situation time to settle instead of making it more difficult?

What can you do in the future to help you let life settle before you react?

PRAYER

Lord, make me slow to speak and slow to become angry. Bathe me in Your wisdom and self-control. God, help me bring You everything. Let my life and reactions go through Your filter of sacrifice, of love, of mercy, of forgiveness, and of Your will. Give me the blessing of letting things clear, and let me say, "First, I will bring it to the Lord." Forgive me for my past reactions and the pain I have caused others by stomping through muddy water. Let Your love cover over my multitude of sins. Settle me, Lord. Amen.

This Is Gossip, Not Prayer

> My dear brothers and sisters, take note of this: Everyone should be quick to listen, slow to speak, and slow to become angry.—James 1:19

> A gossip betrays a confidence, but a trustworthy person keeps a secret.—Proverbs 11:13

There are some ugly people out there. You don't have to share anything with anyone. Be careful. Mrs. Nasty Gossip (who married Mr. BetterThanYou Gossip III) and Mrs. Fake Prayer (who married Mr. Self-Righteous Prayer Jr.) often sit next to each other. They are best friends and like to whisper to each other while they are all dressed up in their church clothes. Don't sit next to this pair. They are an ugly, evil mess.

Every single one of the following statements I have heard. It makes me want to punch that person or, at the very least, throw up on them.

- "She walked down the aisle at church when they called for prayer." (Oh my! Why would you tell me that in that voice, that gossipy hissing-snake voice. Not nice at all. No wonder people don't want to go to church and be judged by us hypocrites.)
- "I am sure she wouldn't mind, but I am just telling you this so you can pray for her. Her husband had an affair. But don't tell anyone. It's just a prayer request."
- "He stole money."
- "She was raped."
- "He does drugs."
- "She shouldn't be here."
- "Why is that kid at church?"
- "Do you think he is even a Christian?"
- "The pastor had an affair."
- "She is pregnant."
- "You shouldn't be here."

And on and on.
Shut your mouth! Close your ears! Run away from gossip!

REFLECTION

Have you ever shared a prayer request wrapped in gossip?

Have you been the one talked about through a gossip chain?

How can you forgive yourself and others?

What can you do in the future not to participate in prayer/church gossip?

How can you avoid being gossiped about when you are in pain?

PRAYER

Lord, forgive us. Forgive me for talking about others when I should stay silent. Lord, let me forgive others when they talk about me and my family. Lord, in 1 Peter 4:8 it says, "Above all, love each other deeply, because love covers over a multitude of sins." Cover us, Lord. Cover our sins. God, prevent me from ever revealing someone's secrets. Shut my mouth from gossip. Protect me from gossip. I ask this in the mighty name of Jesus. Amen.

Balm of Gilead

> Is there no balm in Gilead? Is there no physician there? Why then is there no healing for the wound of my people?
> —Jeremiah 8:22

When you are deeply wounded and your flesh (emotional or literal) is wounded, you need to put some bandages on. You need some salve. You need some of the Holy Spirit's balm of Gilead salve for your wounds. You need the balm of Gilead to go deep into your hurt, your cracks, and your pain and heal you. You are in intensive care. Intensive care units limit visitors to only family. Limiting exposure to others helps you heal. Often, I have heard people pray for the balm of Gilead to heal them or others. There is an old spiritual song about the balm of Gilead. It seems like a special balm, a healing from the Holy Spirit. The Holy Spirit can heal us. In my mind, I can hear this song, and it makes me want to sway and join in the chorus.

There is a balm in Gilead,
There is a balm in Gilead,
To make the wounded whole.
There is a balm in Gilead
To heal the sin-sick soul.
Sometimes I feel discouraged
And leave my fear away.
In prayers, the Holy Spirit
Revives my soul again.
There is a balm in Gilead
To make the wounded whole.
There is a balm in Gilead
To heal the sin-sick soul.
If you can't pray like Peter,
If you can't be like Paul,
Go home and tell your neighbor
He died to save us all.
There is a balm in Gilead

To make the wounded whole.
There is a balm in Gilead
To heal the wounded soul.

What exactly is the balm of Gilead? You have got to love Amazon. You can go to Amazon's website right now and order a "balm of Gilead" salve or oil. We live in an amazing world. Balm of Gilead is traditionally used as a soothing balm for comforting minor discomforts and arthritis, and it is a healing salve. This song and any prayers for the healing power of the balm of Gilead is beautiful. We all want to be whole and to become everything we were created to be. Minor and major discomforts, mistakes, terrible memories, sin, cancer, sickness, and disease are our wounds that need to be healed. We need healing salve for our sin-sick souls. The balm of Gilead in this song, and praying for the healing power of the balm of Gilead, is the Holy Spirit in salve form. The balm in the form of the Holy Spirit is healing, comforting, soothing, and holding. It is for keeping us healthy, making us healthy, and most importantly protecting us. Salve does two things well: keeps the good stuff in and keeps the bad stuff out.

We all need the Holy Spirit balm of Gilead: rare, pure, holy, and healing. God's balm keeps the good stuff in and the bad stuff out.

REFLECTION

What does the balm of Gilead mean to you?

How can you apply the Holy Spirit's balm of Gilead to your life and relationships?

When you are in intensive care, do you think it is wise to limit your exposure to others (even if they are well-meaning)?

Are you willing to let the Holy Spirit comfort you? How?

PRAYER

Jesus, we ask You for the balm of Gilead to heal us. Heal our hearts, minds, and souls. Jesus, heal our memories. Let Your Holy Spirit bind up our wounds and make us everything You created us to be. Protect us, Lord. Amen.

I Can See

> Open the eyes of their hearts, and let the light of Your truth flood in. Shine Your light on the hope You are calling them to embrace. Reveal to them the glorious riches You are preparing as their inheritance.
> —Ephesians 1:18 (Voice)

Right now, I am blindsided. I can't see. I'm not sure what to do. I don't know who to trust. Being able to see is a gift from God. We all have literal vision and spiritual vision. We need both.

When my youngest was little, he was pretending to be Kung Fu Panda, twirling a stick in his hands and doing all the kung fu moves. By accident he scraped his eye severely, at which point he closed his eyes and kept them closed because it hurt too bad to open them. It was as if he was blind. He would not open his eyes. In the house, in the car, and in the waiting room at the hospital, his eyes were sealed shut. Once we finally got to see the doctor, who put pain preventive medicine in his eyes, my son exclaimed loudly, "I can see. I thought I was blind, but I can see."

Sight is such a gift. We don't really appreciate it until it might be gone. Jesus talks about those with sight being blind and the blind seeing. There is a literal sight and a spiritual sight. Sometimes circumstances in life can make us close our spiritual eyes, causing us to become blind to the truth of God. We can't see, feel, or experience God. The eyes of our heart are closed. Just like the doctor who put pain preventive medicine in my son's eye, we might need to get help to recover from our pain. This can come in the form of others praying for us, seeking counseling, or reading our Bible. It is hard to know whom to trust and whom to get help from. We need wisdom.

Open the eyes of my heart, Lord. Open my spiritual eyes. Help me see You. Show me whom to trust.

REFLECTION

Have you ever been in so much pain that you feel blinded by it? Does it make you feel that you can't trust anyone and your whole life is sour?

Do you believe God can open your spiritual eyes and give you both comfort and wisdom?

PRAYER

Lord, heal me. Forgive me. Lord, open the eyes of my heart. Let the light of Your truth flood in. Shine Your light on the hope You are calling me to embrace. Reveal to me the glorious riches You are preparing as my inheritance. Jesus, remove any false lies or false truths I am choosing to believe. Make me whole. Open my spiritual eyes so I can see You and Your glory all around me. Bring me spiritual discernment. Show me whom to trust and whom to get help from. Amen.

Wisdom

That night God appeared to Solomon and said to him, "Ask for whatever you want Me to give you." Solomon answered God, "You have shown great kindness to David my father and have made me king in his place. Now, Lord God, let Your promise to my father David be confirmed, for You have made me king over a people who are as numerous as the dust of the earth. Give me wisdom and knowledge, that I may lead these people, for who is able to govern this great people of Yours?"
—2 Chronicles 1:7–10

Wisdom is what is going to get you through a difficult time. Wisdom gets you through decisions, such as whom to tell and how to live. Wisdom is a gift from God, and it is what I pray for daily for myself and my loved ones.

Solomon was the wisest man ever to live. When God asked him what He could give him, Solomon asked for wisdom. Wisdom from God is a knowing. It is a peace that passes all understanding. It is what I believe some people say is their gut feeling. Unlike Solomon, we have the Holy Spirit available to us. When we ask God, Jesus, and the Holy Spirit to give us wisdom, They give it to us abundantly in wave after wave. I think the best thing besides praying to love God with all our hearts, minds, and souls is to pray for wisdom. Wisdom prevents us from making mistakes, from dating the wrong person to taking the wrong job. It teaches us to be as innocent as doves and as wise as serpents. Life can be tough. If we follow the spirit of the world, it can be dangerous and harmful. To me, wisdom is like divine protection and guidance for how to live one's best life.

We need wisdom. We need God. Show us Your ways, Lord.

REFLECTION

What is the difference between worldly wisdom and wisdom from God?

Do you pray for the fear of the Lord, which is the beginning of wisdom?

PRAYER

Lord, it says in Proverbs 9:10, "The fear of the Lord is the beginning of wisdom, and knowledge of the Holy One is understanding." Lord, I ask You for the fear of the Lord to be in my life. God, I ask You for the Holy One to give me understanding. Bind the fear of the Lord and the Holy One, who gives me understanding in my heart, soul, and mind. Show me what to do and whom to get help from. Most of all, thank You for being the Great Counselor. Amen.

CONCLUSION OF SECTION III

As we conclude the devotions about whom to share things with, let's remember that God is good. He will give us wisdom and will put the right people in our lives at just the right time. God will give us His discretion. Wait for it, and while you wait, give yourself grace.

Section IV

GRACE

After you have stepped in a mess and decided whom to share your mess with, you need to give yourself grace. You need to give others grace. You need to be surrounded by grace and mercy.

Grace and mercy to you, because I see mercy slow dancing, with grace's head on mercy's shoulder and with you being surrounded by their song and comforted by the love they bring.

On the following pages you will find devotions to help you find grace.

Adored

> And He said: "Truly, I tell you, unless you change and become like little children, you will never enter the kingdom of heaven."
> —Matthew 18:3

As grace and mercy dance in your soul, they are singing out to you about God's love for you. You are the apple of His eye. You are adored. Listen to His voice. Embrace the truth. God wants you to know He loves you. He wants you to become like an adored, safe, cared-for little child full of love, joy, and trust.

Have you ever thought about why God makes babies and little ones so adorable? People stop and coo over them, old men go soft and play peekaboo in restaurants, and the babies just look around at who else is going to think they are great. I love it! Have you ever felt so loved that it is like your cup is overflowing with the goodness of God? It is beautiful to see little children when they have that sweet, beautiful look on their faces that says, *I am an adored little child.* This is how God wants us to feel all the time. He wants us to know how incredibly loved we are. He takes the time to count each one of our hairs. He wants to be our best friend. He tells us in Matthew 18:3 to become like little children. How great is that? Trust Me, cuddle up in My arms, let Me count your hairs—I love you and adore you. Bask in God's love, mercy, and grace.

Pray for others and yourself to feel so loved by God that you all become like sweet innocent kind children of God. That is 90 percent of the battle. If you feel loved—if you know you are loved—then you will be free to love. Hey—fact flash—God loves you! Right now! Just as you are! You are adorable. Bask in His glory. The Creator of heaven, of earth, and of you, loves you!

REFLECTION

Will you allow God to surround you in grace and mercy?

Do you truly understand how much God loves you?

PRAYER

Lord, love is all we need. You adore us. You want us to feel both lovable and loved. God, sometimes there is such a heavy feeling of sin in our world, and I and my loved ones feel unloved and unworthy of Your grace, forgiveness, and love. We feel as if we could never be forgiven or worthy of Your love. Forgive us for listening to the lies of the enemy. I ask that Your Holy Spirit surround me and that my loved ones and I feel the love of God. Let us receive Your forgiveness, mercy, and grace, and most of all let us know the love of God. Hug us, Lord. Even when we want to beat on Your chest like spoiled children, let us then fall into Your arms and be cuddled by You. Lord, remove the lies of the devil that tell us we don't deserve to love and that we are unlovable. God, it says in the Bible that nothing can separate us from Your love. I thank You for the truth in Romans 8:38–39: "And I am convinced that nothing can ever separate us from God's love. Neither death nor life, neither angels nor demons, neither our fears for today nor our worries about tomorrow—not even the powers of hades can separate us from God's love. No power in the sky above or in the earth below—indeed, nothing in all creation will ever be able to separate us from the love of God that is revealed in Christ Jesus our Lord" (NLT). Lord, thank You that nothing separates us from Your love. Lord, pour Your anointing of grace and love all over us. Let us know You adore us. Let us frolic like beautiful, happy, loved children. In Jesus's name. Amen.

Details

> The Lord directs the steps of the godly. He delights in every detail of their lives.
> —Psalm 37:23 (NLT)

When you live in grace, you know God is in the details, the nitty-gritty everyday details. Yes, He is there in the monumental moments of your life, but He loves you so much that He also cares about every tiny second of your day. God really cares about all of you, every little detail.

Have you ever been in a Bible study, small group, or Sunday school class that is sharing a prayer request and someone just drops a doozy such as "My husband just left me" or "My kid has cancer"? Huge. Overwhelming. Life-changing. On-one's-knees sort of prayers, the kind of prayers that stay with you all day long and into the night. You wake up and pray; you drive and pray; and even when you talk to others, you still cry out to God in your heart for this prayer request. Then in the back of your mind, you think about the prayer request you were going to share. It is important, but not as important as those prayers, so you just stay silent. You still pray about it, but it seems so petty that you almost feel bad about asking.

If you have felt bad about your own prayer request because someone else's seemed "bigger," then this is where you are wrong—so very wrong! God cares about all of it. Look at nature. He puts the black spots on a red ladybug, fuzzy legs on a caterpillar, intricate designs on a butterfly, and the great wild roar in a lion. He knows it all. He watches every breath you breathe. He counts the hairs on your head, every single one. This kind of love is detailed, personal, and vulnerable! God wants to share everything from "What's for dinner?" to "Could you please heal me from this disease?" He cares about where you plant a flower and how you treat your family. He cares about what you eat and how you drive. He loves every single detail of you and wants to be a part of it all. He wants your fellowship. He did not send His Son to die on the cross just for the big parts of your life. He sent His Son to die on the cross so he could have an intimate relationship with you. All of you.

God cares about every little detail of you, from how your cells work to the number of hairs on your head. He cares about how the Earth rotates to provide sunshine just for you. He is about relationships. God is there for you, not just for the big doozies, but for all the details of your life and the lives of your loved ones. He is a best friend who wants to sit on the couch with a good cup of tea and visit. He wants to be your best friend, on the same page, buddies, of the same cloth, kindred spirits, and united: "But whoever is united with the Lord is one with Him in spirit" (1 Corinthians 6:17).

REFLECTION

In your close relationships, do you spend time with your loved ones only when they or you need something, or do you enjoy just being together?

Are you comfortable talking to God about everything?

Do you realize God loves you and wants to be with you?

PRAYER

Lord, You want to know all of me. Teach me to be with You all day long in conversation. Help me to be thankful and joyful, knowing that You care about every little detail of my life and the lives of others. You are in the details. Love is in the details. Your grace is in the details. I will trust in You for the big, the little, and all that is in between. I love You, Lord. Thank You, God. Amen.

Shine

> Therefore, I tell you, her many sins have been forgiven—as her great love has shown. But whoever has been forgiven little loves little.
> —Luke 7:47

Grace never gives up. Even in pain, hurt, and misery, grace can still win. Grace is like Powerade for the soul. It gets you through. You don't know what a good day is until you have experienced some bad days. For those of us who have experienced some dark places, I think we appreciate the light more. When we leave sin, mistakes, hardships, and tragedies behind, we know for certain we don't want to go back. We know how bad it can be. We remember what it was like when it was dark and wicked, and now we cling to Jesus so much that we start to reflect His love. We shine.

"That is their story. Sometimes those who have hurt the most are the ones who truly know what it means to love. The more we are forgiven and rescued, the brighter we shine." This was the answer my dear friend gave me when I expressed my sorrow about the pain that I saw in the eyes of the three- and four-year-olds at the homeless shelter where we were working. It broke my heart. This wise counsel got me through the morning without tears. It gave me hope and knowledge that God is in charge, and therefore I could just love, play, and bring joy to those children's hard world. Later that day God was very sweet to me. I was in my Bible at Luke 7:41–43:

"Two people owed money to a certain moneylender. One who owed him five hundred denarii, and the other fifty. Neither of them had the money to pay him back, so he forgave the debts of both. Now which of them loved him more? Simon replied, 'I suppose the one who had the bigger debt forgiven.' 'You have judged correctly,' Jesus said."

On this page in my Bible I wrote, "God is a God of miracles. The ones rescued from the most darkness shine the brightest." I also underlined and starred the verse Luke 7:47:

"Therefore, I tell you, her many sins have been forgiven—as her great love has shown. But he who has been forgiven little loves little."

God is a God of miracles. He can take our darkest memories, our regrets, our pain, and our struggles and make them into something beautiful. Don't you worry, friend, if you feel you have gotten a raw deal. I truly believe because of that raw deal—either done to you or arising from your own choices—you can be redeemed. God is a God of miracles! He can take the worst and make it something beautiful. It says in Psalm 30:11, "You have turned my mourning into joyful dancing. You have taken away my clothes of mourning and clothed me with joy" (ESV).

Here is the deal, though: you have got to be vulnerable in front of God, take off your mourning clothes, expose yourself—all of you—to God, and let Him clothe you with His love and joy. Go on. Let go. Get real and then get clothed with joy! Shine the brightest. Nothing is impossible with God. He can redeem any situation and place you in His glorious light!

REFLECTION

Are you willing to be raw with God? Write down the 'mourning clothes' you need to discard:

Do you know that God is the God of not only second chances, but also of third to infinity chances? Do you believe this? Why or why not?

PRAYER

God, I know that nothing is impossible for You. If You can take a man like Saul, who killed Christians, and change his name to Paul who learns to love Jesus and ends up writing a good portion of the New Testament, then You can do anything. You can raise the dead, like You did Lazarus. You have prostitutes in the family genealogy of Christ. You are our Redeemer! Even when humans mean things for evil, You bring good out of it as You did when Joseph was sold into slavery by his brothers and then became the very one who redeemed his family from starvation as the second-in-command of all of Egypt. Darkness is not even dark to You. In Psalm 139:12 it says, "Even darkness will not be dark to You; the night will shine like day, for darkness is as light to You." You have the final say. You can redeem us all. Thank

You, God, that nothing is impossible for You. I lift all of Your children in pain to Your holy throne room. The shofar (a ram's horn that is blown in the synagogue) blows and declares, "Enough." Your mighty love, mercy, grace, and power prevail! In Jesus's holy name. You get the final say.

You are the Redeemer! Mighty grace wins! Amen!

Laws to Love

> But if there is serious injury, you are to take life for life, eye for eye, tooth for tooth, hand for hand, foot for foot, burn for burn, wound for wound, bruise for bruise.
> —Exodus 21:23–25

Grace from Jesus changes who we are. It takes the mean law of following the manipulative ways of humankind and blows it to pieces with a gigantic grace bomb. Because I have siblings, I experienced some serious hate around the age of ten in the back seat of our car. It's a good thing our parents were in the front, because otherwise my siblings might be dead and I would be in jail for murder. The Old Testament law about taking only an eye for an eye is in place for siblings like me.

In the Old Testament, the rule that you could take only an eye for an eye was a great one and very necessary. Anyone who has had the joy of growing up with siblings understands that this is a necessary law. We humans would take an eye, then a leg, then burn the house down, then wrestle our siblings to the ground and kidnap the dog. Siblings understand this. There must be a stopping point, a truce, a line separating them in the back seat of the car that ain't nobody gonna cross. Then along comes *radical* Jesus, and you get saved.

If anyone forces you to go one mile, go with them two miles. Give to the one who asks you and do not turn away from the one who wants to borrow from you. You have heard that it was said, "Love your neighbor and hate your enemy," but I tell you, love your enemies and pray for those who persecute you, that you may be children of Your Father in heaven. He causes His sun to rise on the evil and the good and sends rain on the righteous and the unrighteous. If you love those who love you, what reward will you get? Are not even the tax collectors doing that? And if you greet only your own people, what are you doing more than others? Do not even pagans do that? Be perfect, therefore, as your heavenly Father is perfect. (Matthew 5:41–48)

No longer do we take an eye for an eye. There is a new boss in town and a better way—a radical, life-changing way. We forgive! We pray for our enemies! We bless those who persecute us! When asked to carry someone's stuff one mile, we gladly and cheerfully carry it two. We don't knee-jerk react anymore. Because we are loved, we love.

It's unfathomable! Insane love! Radical! Our hearts are on fire with the love of Jesus! Let radical Jesus take you from laws to love! Sidenote: I accepted Jesus Christ, my Lord and Savior, at the age of eleven. My siblings made it to adulthood, and they are my favorite people now.

REFLECTION

Ask God if there is a relationship in your life that needs to go from laws to love.

How does grace change you and your circumstances?

PRAYER

Lord, our hearts overflow with Your peace, joy, and love. You fill us with Yourself, and we will never thirst again. Lord, may Your love overflow from our hearts to others. Because You love us, we can love. Use us. Give us this wonderful uncontainable love for others. Thank You for Your grace that makes love possible. Amen.

Hurts

As it is written: "None is righteous, no, not one."
—Romans 3:10 (ESV)

Grace won't let me look in the mirror and fail to see my own flaws. You have hurt me, and I have done the hurting. You have judged me, and I have done the judging. You have talked about me, and I have done the talking. You have gossiped, and I have told.

"Why do you look at the speck of sawdust in your brother's eye and pay no attention to the plank in your own eye? How can you say to your brother, 'Let me take the speck out of your eye,' when all the time there is a plank in your own eye? You hypocrite, first take the plank out of your own eye, and then you will see clearly to remove the speck from your brother's eye" (Matthew 7:3–5).

All I can do in situations of pain is to pray and ask God for mercy, mercy for me, mercy for those I have hurt, mercy for those who have hurt me, and mercy to stop the pain and harmful cycles. We are all sinful humans. We need grace and we need to give grace.

REFLECTION

How can God's grace help you to forgive and ask for forgiveness?

Are you willing to look in the mirror and find grace for yourself and others?

What do you see when you look in your own eyes?

PRAYER

Lord, I ask for forgiveness for my judgmental spirit. Destroy my judgmental spirit in me. It is Yours to judge, not me. Lord, forgive me when I have hurt, gossiped, and judged. God, take the plank out of me. Lord, let me be quick to love and forgive others. Let me not offend others or take offense. Cleanse me from all unrighteousness. You are God and I am not. Please Lord, make this right in Your eyes. Amen.

Not My Will, but Yours Be Done

> Two men, both criminals, were also led out with Him to be executed. When they came to the place called the Skull, there they crucified Him, along with the criminals, one on His right, the other on His left. Jesus said, "Father forgive them, for they do not know what they are doing." And they divided up His clothes by casting lots.
> —Luke 23:32–34

To get through life, you need lots of grace—grace that goes ahead and forgives people before they even hurt you. How in the world do you get that kind of unworldly grace? Look at Luke 22, where Jesus wept tears of blood and said, "Not My will, but Yours be done."

That is a hard thing to say and even a harder thing to live, especially if you have experienced tragedy and had no choice in the matter.

Life can be hard. Unfair hair. As I listened to a friend with tears running down his face telling me all the cruel things he had experienced and all the explanations people had given him for the awful, heartbreaking, life-changing tragedy of losing his children in an accident two years previously, my heart hurt. With my heart, time, and prayers, I was trying to help him through this. I asked him to understand that people rarely know what to say. They get nervous and just start talking. They want to help, to love others through such difficult times, but often they end up being hurtful instead. I begged him to forgive others before they hurt him, to offer grace. People can be dumb and say mean things, but most of the time they are just trying to help in their own human way. Their intentions are good; their delivery, not so much. I'm not sure my friend understood. I was struggling with my own hurts and the pain of forgiving myself and others for having said ugly things. For me, "Not my way, Your way" is the key to being able to say, "God forgive them and me. We don't know any better." Jesus asked that the cup be taken from Him and then submitted to the will of God.

Sometimes when I pray, I wonder if I am praying God's will. When I am on a walk, I pray and talk through things with God. I can be angry, hurt, full of praise, desperate, or thankful. I express all of it to God. I often pray that God will help me pray for His will. I sometimes really let it out. I think I obsess over things, people, or situations that I should just let go of. Sometimes I don't even trust that my prayers reflect God's will. My safety net is to pray "Not my way, but Your way." With this, I cover it all. It is as if I have had a good heart-to-heart with God, letting Him know it all and then trusting Him with it all.

When Jesus asked God to forgive them, He didn't say who to forgive. He didn't explain who the "them" was. To me, it is easier to forgive the mocking criminals and the guys who are casting lots for his clothes. They don't know any better. But God is good, and I think the "them" are all of us: the religious people who are supposed to love God and His followers; Jesus's friends, who are supposed to have His back; the crowd, who are supposed to let the innocent go free; and the criminals who are supposed to die for their sins.

The "them" is me and you. I think Jesus had decided ahead of time to forgive when He gave it all to God. That is when the "forgive them" took place. I believe that if we pray "Not my will, but Yours be done," we will be blessed with the same "forgive them" attitude before we can even become offended. So, my prayer is "Not my will, but Yours be done," and my praise is that through this submission I can forgive "them" before it even happens, while it is happening, and after it happens. The "them" is all of it and all of us. Only grace makes this possible.

REFLECTION

Are you willing to have so much grace and trust in God that you can decide ahead of time to forgive others before they even hurt you?

If you could forgive others before they hurt you, write down how that could change your life.

PRAYER

Lord, not my will, but Yours be done. I forgive others through You before it happens, while it is happening, and after is happening. I am crucified with Christ. Your love and grace protect me. Amen.

Pigs Don't Wear Pearls

> Do not give dogs what is sacred; do not throw your pearls to pigs. If you do, they may trample them under their feet and turn and tear you to pieces.
> —Matthew 7:6

It's okay to walk away and give yourself grace. You are never going to please everyone. Ever. Some people are just pigs and will just keep taking. Be smart. Relationships can be messy. Sometimes you pick your friends and it's mutual, and sometimes you get picked or forced into a relationship. If the relationship is a life drainer, you can put healthy boundaries around it. Some people are fountains, and some people are drains.

There is a relationship in my life that I am tired of. It has just worn me out. After years of giving, listening, and being bombarded by this relationship, I need to put a pig fence around it and stop giving it my precious time, resources, and attention. I will always be kind, but no longer will I let this person come into my life and trample me. The verse at the head of this chapter is harsh but true. Sometimes there are people in your life who take your pearls and trample you. You give and give and give. They trample your gifts, your kindness, and your well-meaning gestures and tear on your heart, your reputation, and your peace. It is time to stop giving them what is sacred—your time, your resources, and your heart. Be wise and set healthy boundaries. Be careful out there. Pigs don't wear pearls.

Life is short. If you have overgiven, it's okay to stay away from hungry, never satisfied, exhausting, manipulative, and unappreciative people. These people are drains.

REFLECTION

Is there a situation or person in your life that you need to put a pig fence around? How can that help both you and the person you need to protect yourself from?

How do you put a pig fence around that situation?

Boundaries are good and can protect you and others. It can release both you and the person you need to protect yourself from. Pray for wisdom. Ask God to cover this situation in His mighty grace.

PRAYER

Holy Father, make me wise. Help me to give myself grace. I ask You for a hedge of protection. In Jesus's name, cancel all evil, all manipulation, and the lies of the enemy from my life. Destroy any unholy bonds or unholy obligations. I serve You, Lord, and only You. "As for me and my house, we will worship the Lord" (Joshua 24:15). Lord, give me Your grace, wisdom, love, and discernment. Amen.

Doing Right by You

> Let us not become weary in doing good, for at the proper time,
> we will reap a harvest if we do not give up.
> —Galatians 6:9 (MSG)

True grace means you do what is right even when you don't feel like it. Gritty grace. It's where the rubber meets the road! Often in life we should do what is right even if we don't feel like it. It can be extremely difficult, but most relationships that are worth anything are worth the difficulty.

My friend Christy is a strong woman. She is articulate, intelligent, and on top of things—beautiful on the inside and outside. She has strong convictions, she is in love with God, and she is a wonderful servant. One of the things I admire about her is that she will tell you like it is. She is the person I like to stand behind and let her say what I am thinking and say, "You go, girl." Ain't nobody messes with Christy! That's the surface. She could intimidate you if you didn't know her like I do. She is so humble and constantly humbles herself before the Lord. She will examine her actions and take action to make relationships right. Sometimes that means choosing to love, forgive, be kind and merciful even if she doesn't feel it. This is where her strong grit comes in! She often says with a smile or a sigh, "Fake it till you make it." The most wonderful thing is that I have seen her "make it" repeatedly. She is obedient to God and what she knows is best and keeps working at it until she makes it. You don't always have to feel all those wonderful fluffy loving feelings to do the right thing. Often, you just chose to do the right thing whether or not you feel it.

It's amazing how it works: you keep doing the right thing over and over and eventually your heart changes, then your perspective changes and sometimes even your circumstances change.

REFLECTION

What rules your relationships—your feelings or doing the right thing? Why?

PRAYER

Lord, You know my heart. I want to do what is right, even if I don't feel like doing what is right. Take over my relationships. Make me strong and loving, even if I am in an emotional storm. Teach me when to say something and when to be silent. Let me pray and show Your love to others, even when they show me hate. Guide and direct me. Heal anyone whom I have hurt. Let me have the beauty of the Lord's presence all around me. Protect me from myself and give me an obedient, strong spirit to do Your will. Cover me in Your mighty grace. Amen.

Purity Falling from Heaven

> "Come now, let us settle the matter," says the Lord. "Though your sins are like scarlet, they shall be as white as snow; though they are red as crimson, they shall be like wool."
> —Isaiah 1:18

Grace, beautiful grace. One grace snowflake after another. We don't have to work hard to be right with God. In fact, it's a total grace thing that we get to be in a relationship with God. It's like delightful grace falling from heaven onto us and covering all our sin and pain.

As I write this, it is snowing outside. Big flakes. The snow covers everything. I can lean my head back and just see huge snowflakes, one after another, dancing down to earth to make all become white. We are being covered in a pure white beautiful blanket. Even what was a rubbish pile is now draped in beauty. In Georgia, this is a treat. We shut down. No school, work, or driving. It becomes quiet, reverent, and then celebratory. Neighbors go for walks, and kids play in pure awe. It is delightful. This is what God can do for us. He can settle the matter. He can take our sins and cancel them with His purity. Not just when it is snowing, but always. We can lean our heads back and bask in His forgiveness, mercy, and love. First it is quiet in our souls, next reverent, and then celebratory. We can delight in this wondrous miracle. We can go out and celebrate with the neighbors. It's snowing!

Let God's grace and mercy cover you. Let God settle the matter between you and Him. Accept His free gift of purity and of being made right.

REFLECTION

Visualize lavish grace being poured on you and your loved ones. Now, how do you live differently because of it?

PRAYER

Lord, nothing is impossible for You. Thank You for settling the matter of sin and separation from You. I throw my head back and look up to the heavens and feel Your forgiveness, purity, and kindness fall on me. You settled the matter on the cross with Jesus dying for my sins. You settled the matter by raising Christ from the dead. You settled the matter of sin and separation. I receive Your gift. I accept. It is settled. Cover me, Lord, in Your grace. Amen.

CONCLUSION OF SECTION IV

Wrap yourself and others in grace for all your days. Grace is a beautiful, life-giving covering. It will make all the difference in your life and the lives of others. Think of grace as a divine blanket from heaven.

CONCLUSION OF SECTION IV

Section V

MOURN

So, you have decided to share or not to share with some of your closest friends. You have wrapped your situation in the grace of God. Now, you need to give yourself time to mourn—mourn what you lost, mourn what was stolen, mourn that life is not what you thought it was going to be.

Get it out. Let yourself cry. Cry it out. It's okay not to understand, to cry, to mourn. You need to mourn; it is part of the process. Not all of life makes sense, and it never will.

On the following pages you will find devotions to help you mourn.

Hacked

He [Jesus] wept.—John 11:35 (KJV)

Every once in a while, you are going along in life thinking about simple things such as what pillows would look nice on your sofa, then suddenly your life gets hacked.

You are blindsided. Shocked. Agony and discord set in. What was your life is now crumbled in pieces around you. You are raw. Every emotion, thought, and action is now superfocused and in overdrive. It is hard just to get through the moment, much less the day.

It is a gift from God that all our moments are not like that, because otherwise I think we would die from the sheer exhaustion of being so sensitive and emotionally exposed. It is as if our guts are hanging out from our lives being hit by a bombshell. But whatever the cause of the pain, I find comfort in the fact that Jesus was both human and God. He hurt down here too. John 11:35 is the shortest divinely human verse in the Bible: "He wept" (KJV).

I am crying, Lord. I hurt too.

REFLECTION

Picture Christ not just crying but weeping—deep sobs, excruciating pain. Allow Him to hold you in His arms while you both weep.

PRAYER

Lord, You hurt too down here when weeping was the only appropriate answer. Hold me while we weep together. Amen.

I Don't Get It

"For My thoughts are not your thoughts, neither are your ways My ways," declares the Lord. "As the heavens are higher than the earth, so are My ways higher than your ways and My thoughts than your thoughts."
—Isaiah 55:8–9

In my tears and sobs, I don't understand. This is hard. Sometimes I just plain don't get it. How can God allow this to happen?

A child drowning, abuse, a miscarriage, unemployment, the tragic death of a person who was way too young, cancer, sickness, war—the list goes on. I do not have a vending machine type of faith. I have lived through and seen tragedy, been angry, grieved, and shaken my fist at heaven, not understanding! *Why? What is the purpose of this?* Life can be unfair and miserable. Utter heartbreak and anger have caused me to yell, "How in the world can good come out of this?" Sometimes there is no neat bow and packaging. Sometimes life is nasty, messy, cruel, unfair, and tragic. There are some things I have lived through on this earth that I will never understand. Ever!

Time does a wonderful thing of softening it all, putting perspective on it, if not providing understanding. Having gone through such difficulty makes you relatable, real, and hopefully kinder and wiser. Sometimes all you can do is just rest in the arms of Jesus and accept that you don't understand everything.

REFLECTION

Does it make you angry that life is so unfair and hard? Why?

What do you do with your pain, your not understanding, and the tragedies that happen to you?

PRAYER

Lord, Your ways and thoughts are higher than my ways and thoughts. I am stuck here in a sin-stained world. I don't understand sometimes. You are not so small that I can understand all Your ways. You are God and I am not. It will take me my complete life and beyond to know You. I rest in Your arms. Hold me while I weep. Amen.

Bring Us Godly Sorrow

> Godly sorrow brings repentance that leads to salvation and leaves no regret, but worldly sorrow brings death.
> —2 Corinthians 7:10

While you mourn, make sure it is godly sorrow you are feeling.

Godly sorrow is full of a love that leads into the arms of Jesus and takes away your sin, cancels regret, and holds you. Life is not always fair or understandable, and because we are human, we mess up. Godly sorrow opens the door to peace, joy, and a life of blessings and a relationship with your Creator. Worldly sorrow condemns you, haunts you, takes away your peace and joy, and leads you to make bad choices (very bad choices).

Godly sorrow comforts you and lets you know it will be okay. You are being held in the arms of God. Worldly sorrow offers no grace, only shame and condemnation.

REFLECTION

It is okay to have deep sorrow, regret, and pain. Work through it.

Read Romans 8:1 How can you protect yourself from worldly sorrow?

PRAYER

Jesus, bring us and our loved ones only godly sorrow that brings repentance that leads to salvation and leaves no regret. Amen!

The One He Loves

Near the cross of Jesus stood His mother, and His mother's sister, Mary, the wife of Clopas, and Mary Magdalen. When Jesus saw His mother there, and the disciple whom He loved standing nearby, He said to His mother, "Dear woman, here is your son." Then He said to the disciple, "Here is your mother." And from that hour that disciple took her to his own home.
—John 19:25–27

When you are mourning, you need to remember who you are and whose you are! You are the one God loves.

If you read the Bible, you will find there are many entertaining characters in it. John is one of them. He wrote the book of John, and in that book he describes himself in the third person as the one whom Jesus loved. That is so endearing. John was Jesus's faithful friend, an I-can-be-trusted-and-I've-got-your-back kind of friend. He is like the quiet, faithful, non-show-off friend who is there for you.

When all the other disciples had deserted Jesus, John stood beneath the cross with Jesus's mother. When you have a friend that is so close and so loyal that your family is like their family and their family is like your family, and you deeply care for one another and each other's well-being, that is when you know you are loved. It is something special. You don't need to put your name in the spotlight, but rather your relationship: the one whom He loved. That says it all.

Want to know something? You also are the one whom Jesus loves. His love is now, in the present, expressed on the cross and sealed with the Holy Spirit. Accept it. Say it. Live it. Claim it. When you know you are loved, you can love and be lovable. Start describing yourself as "the one whom Jesus loves" because that is exactly who you are.

REFLECTION

Do you think that because you are in pain and mourning, Jesus doesn't love you? If so, why do you think that?

How would describing yourself as the one whom Jesus loves change you?

PRAYER

Lord, let my heart be like John's, and let me describe myself as the one whom Jesus loves. I don't need my name in the spotlight, but I do need our relationship. That is who I am: the one Jesus loves. Thank You, for in John 3:16 this truth screams out: "For God so loved the world that He gave His one and only Son, that whoever believes in Him shall not perish but have eternal life." Thank you, Lord, that I am the one whom Jesus loves. Amazing! Unfathomable! Received! Amen.

Hug Them, Lord

> But God demonstrates His own love for us in this: While we were still sinners, Christ died for us.—Romans 5:8

Sometimes during the mourning process, you just need God to hug you or hug the one you love who is in deep mourning. It is very hard to see someone who is utterly broken and without hope, especially someone whom you love dearly.

Recently I have been praying for someone, and all I can pray is for God to hug them. They are so hurt, angry, defensive, and broken that they need the Lord to hug them and let them know that they are loved. "Right now, hug them, hug them just as they are, Lord." Love prevails. Hear this in your heart, mind, and soul: "You are loved. Loved. Loved. Loved. Just as you are." "He heals the brokenhearted and binds up their wounds" (Psalm 147:3 ESV). Nothing is impossible with God. Prayer goes places we can't. We can pray, and pray we shall! God gives us hope and gives hope to others.

REFLECTION

If Christ died for us while we are sinners, do we really need to be in the "right place" for Christ to love us just as we are? Why?

PRAYER

Lord, You heal the brokenhearted and bind up their wounds. Thank You, God, that you are not afraid of messiness. Heal _____ [your name or the person you are praying for]. You love _____! While _____ is still a sinner, Christ died for _____. Hug _____ tight. Comfort _____. Take away all the lies of the devil from _____. In Jesus's name, may nothing separate _____ from You.

Ashes for Beauty

> To all who mourn in Israel, He will give a crown of beauty for ashes, a joyous blessing instead of mourning, festive praise instead of despair. In their righteousness, they will be like great oaks that the Lord has planted for His own glory.
> —Isaiah 61:3 (NLT)

I came to God in my despair with my mourning clothes on. Ash and soot were all over me. I was broken. He sat me down, and we had a long visit. He washed me clean and dressed me in white. My broken dreams and disappointments were real, but somehow I finally became the one who was real, and in that realness, I became more beautiful than I ever thought possible. Mourn as long as you need, but after a while, you are going to want to trade ashes for beauty. It's exhausting being miserable and unhappy, and it's especially exhausting being around miserable and unhappy people. It's just not fun. When I realize this, I don't want to mourn anymore. I become tired of me.

To all who mourn because of broken dreams, death, disappointments, sickness, despair, He will give a crown of beauty for ashes. The ashes mean that something is so bad that it is burned up. Gone. Broken. Beyond repair. A crown of beauty is pure, beautiful, and full of honor and joy, meaning one is restored, set apart for glory—a joyous blessing instead of mourning. As if a blessing weren't enough, it is going to be a joyous blessing. Joyous: happy, light, easy, delightful. Blessing: great, more than you could ask for, undeserved! A joyous blessing instead of mourning. A joyous blessing instead of misery, sadness, and despair. Okay. Deal. Festive praise instead of despair. Festive: party, fun, good time. Praise: thankfulness, adoration, abandonment of self instead of despair, depression, sadness, and hopelessness. Festive praise instead of despair. Wow.

"In their righteousness, they will be like great oaks that the Lord has planted for His own glory." God takes death and all our broken dreams, disappointments, sickness, and despair and gives us a crown of beauty for our ashes. Then He gives us happiness, light, delightfulness beyond blessings. He gives us joyous blessings for mourning. Instead of sadness, misery, and despair, He gives us a festive party, a good time, thankfulness, adoration, and abandonment of self. Abandonment of self is so great. You actually love and care for others now. It is awesome. You are finally free from your hurts and bondage, even if they are as real as the air you breathe. The hurts just don't keep you in bondage anymore. You realize that this earth we are living on is just temporary. We will be in eternity with all our sadness and pain destroyed in just a short while. Because of the righteousness, the grace, and the peace that passes all understanding we can receive from Him, He makes us become like strong oaks planted for His glory. We display God's glory, knowing soon, soon, my friend, we will be with God. Our branches and our lives look upward to the heavens. Thank You, God! Receive it. God has the last word.

Strong oaks can weather storms. Strong oaks did not get strong by way of everything being perfect. Strong oaks are wise and solid, and their roots go deep. Strong oaks have been around a long time and have seen it all. They reproduce and make a beautiful forest. Strong oaks know that nothing lasts forever. There are seasons of hurt, pain, joy, love, and loss. The oaks have branches for swinging and for building forts. They stand out. They feed the forest. Need I go on? For Your glory, God!

REFLECTION

Mourning should be only for a season. Many times, the pain will be with you forever. How can you grow and become stronger from your pain and sadness?

Do you think you could use your pain to glorify God? How?

PRAYER

Heavenly Father, through the power that raised Jesus from the dead, I ask for You to give me a crown of beauty for ashes, a joyous blessing instead of mourning, and festive praise instead of despair. Because You make me righteous, make me like a great oak that the Lord has planted for Your own glory. I abandoned self-misery and chose You instead. It is still hard and hurts, but in that hardness and hurt, You make my roots grow deep. This is for Your glory! I am beautiful in the pain. I am strong, like a righteous oak. Amen.

CONCLUSION OF SECTION V

Mourning and crying are good for the soul. It is the way the soul releases its deepest pain—through teardrops and deep sobs.

As we conclude the devotions about mourning, we acknowledge that sometimes our sadness turns to anger, and that is okay. If we don't mourn for what we have lost, then we go straight to anger, with sobs and tears still caught in our souls. It's all a process, so continue to wrap yourself and others in blankets of grace. Don't be afraid of processing through your mourning and anger.

Section VI

ANGRY

I am angry!

Even after you trade your ashes for beauty, your heart can still hurt, and you can be angry in this hurt. Sometimes you may be afraid of anger, but unless you are honest about your anger, you aren't really going to get better.

Don't be afraid of anger. God knows your thoughts and wants to help you process them. Be honest with God. He can handle your anger. Get angry, question, make it real.

God can handle it.
If you bury this anger instead of wrestling it to the ground, it's going to seep out somewhere. It seeps out most often on your insides and makes you ugly and coldhearted. Or your anger blows up on innocent bystanders and sprays them with manipulative cruelty. It is okay to be angry. It is okay to recognize your hurt and disappointment. It is good to ask God to take your anger and show you what to do with it.

Anger is an emotion you need to nurse. It is dangerous and can be toxic. It can stick to your insides and change you and dangerously hurt others. What you do with your anger and how you handle it is going to determine if you allow God to use it for good or if you will become an awful version of yourself. Work through this. Take your time. Make your anger make you better, not bitter. At the beginning of the devotions, we will address anger. Then we can be angry at those who hurt us, then angry at ourselves. And finally I am going to ask you to leave anger behind. Leave it behind even if your life and what caused the anger still doesn't make sense.

On the following pages you will find devotions
to help you work through anger.

Why I Think We Have Cusswords

> Therefore, just as sin came into the world through one man, and death through sin, and so death spread to all men because all sinned.
> —Romans 5:12 (CSB)

Right now, I am so angry that I want to scream every dirty word I know. Life is just heavy and full of disgusting sin sometimes. There is no other way to describe it.

Sometimes I cuss. I have prayed that I will stop. It's not attractive. These four-letter words seem to be connected to a voice box that has its own agenda, especially when I drop something heavy on my foot. When I worked in a retirement home, several of the Alzheimer's patients couldn't complete sentences, but they could cuss. There was this one retired preacher who let it rip all the time. You could hear those four-letter words from down the hall. The same thing happened to my father-in-law after his stroke. Maybe it is because things like that are awful and make one feel like cussing. But for me, I know better. And know it's bad to cuss, but sometimes I think I need to say an ugly word to get my point across. It is more emphatic and gets others' attention better than saying, "The manure I just stepped in finds me in an extremely unpleasant state of mind." Maybe I should try that instead. It might make me, and others, laugh.

Here is my point: down here in these earthly realms, there can be a lot of heartbreak—broken promises, poverty, out-of-whack hormones, sickness, accidents, mistakes, death, betrayal, misunderstandings, and tragedy, just to mention some. Lots of times there are just nasty, smelly, hurt feelings and bad situations. When Adam and Eve had to leave the garden, I think that is when bad words found their way into humans' vocabulary.

We live in a sinful, fallen world. We no longer walk in the garden with God. Sin is heavy and all around us now, like a thick layer of fog. I bet right after Adam and Eve realized what they'd done when they ate the apple, they didn't say, "Oh me, oh my!"

REFLECTION

Jesus got angry. Think about Him in the temple driving out the money changers. We live in a sinful, fallen world. Does *all* sin make you angry? Why?

PRAYER

Lord, sometimes it feels so thick with sin on this earth that I feel as if cussing is the only way to express how I feel. I hate sin, and it makes me angry. I'm angry at the sin in me and around me. I live in a fallen, sinful world. I experience the consequences of sin. I daily must die to myself and my ways and remind myself that my flesh is dead and only Jesus lives through me. Lord, I am reminded of what they said at my grandmother's funeral: "The daily struggle of living in the flesh and surrendering to Christ is over. She is with Christ." I look forward to that day when I am with Christ. For now, I intentionally die to my fleshly sinful ways and keep putting You in charge. Repeatedly. I utterly depend upon You. Amen.

Vengeance

> Do not take revenge, my dear friends, but leave room for God's wrath, for it is written: "It is mine to avenge; I will repay," says the Lord.
> —Romans 12:19

When you are angry, you want justice. You want things to be made right. You want someone to pay. You want vengeance! Have you ever been so angry that you just want to tackle the situation to the ground and stomp on it? Pull someone's hair or at least mess it up? Do you want to punish the perpetrator for his or her crime? Wouldn't that feel great?

"Vengeance is Mine, thus saith the Lord" is said best King James style. Sometimes when I am really upset about an awful situation that needs some fixing up, I just repeat, "Vengeance is Mine, thus saith the Lord." It feels good for me to say it. I like to say it with a slight aristocratic English accent and pretend I have a robe on and a sword in my hand. It feels good to scream, "Vengeance is Mine, thus saith the Lord!" I will totally admit that I usually don't say it lovingly. More than likely, I say it when I am hurt and angry. But then I remember what a wise friend once told me: "When you feel like it is your responsibility to punish someone, you are carrying a heavy burden." This desire to punish those who have hurt me puts a thick layer of ugliness on me. It's like lugging around a burdensome ax that is so heavy and so overwhelming that it is all I think about. It changes my personality for the worse. It makes me grumpy, causes me to lose sleep, and overwhelms me. It's all-consuming. But as my dear friend explained, when you lay down the ax and give the burden to God, you are free! And with a sly smile, she reminded me that God can do a much better job of punishing the wrongdoer than I can. So, I lay down the ax. I am not the judge and never will be. And what if I am wrong about the situation or that person? And I become angry and mean and spend my life trying to punish them? Not my job. What a waste of my life! When you give it to God—even with an aristocratic English accent—He does what is right.

Whew, what a relief! I am now free to be a happy, cared-for child of

God. He's got my back! When I feel my anger rise, I just repeat, "Vengeance is Mine, thus saith the Lord! Go get 'em, Lord!"

REFLECTION

It is okay and normal to be angry. It's what you do with the anger that can be dangerous. Will you lay down your ax and allow God to deliver the vengeance? Write down your "ax'.

PRAYER

Lord, I am angry. What just happened is not right. It is not just. I am angry. Angry. Why? How? This is not right. It is wrong! Lord, I don't have the eyes or the wisdom to see this like You do. All I can say is, I give You this situation. Go get them, Lord. Take care of all of it. I release myself from this anger, and I totally give it to You. It is in Your throne room. My hands, feelings, and emotions are off. Thank You, God, for taking this from me. Thank You, Lord, for doing what is right. Thank You for protecting me from myself and protecting me and my loved ones from others. Lord, You are trustworthy and I trust You. No matter what. You have the final say. Always. Amen.

Go Get 'Em

> You have heard that it was said, love your neighbor and hate your enemy, but I tell you, love your enemies and pray for those who persecute you, that you may be children of your Father in heaven. He causes His sun to rise on the evil and the good and sends rain on the righteous and the unrighteous. If you love those who love you, what reward will you get? Are not even the tax collectors doing that? And if you greet only your own people, what are you doing more than others? Do not even the pagans do that? Be perfect, therefore, as your heavenly Father is perfect.
> —Matthew 5:43–48

Much easier said than done. Loving and praying for your enemies is hard, then wonderful. And then it becomes miraculous!

It is beneficial to the soul to say and pray, "Vengeance is Mine thus saith the Lord." Remind yourself often that it is not your job to punish others. When you release your vengeance to God, an amazing miracle happens. By releasing the job of delivering vengeance to God, you can freely say, "Go get 'em, God." When you say "Go get 'em, God," your heart changes and you find yourself praying for blessings, for healing, and for your enemies to truly know the love of the Lord. You end up going round and round in these circles of prayer and praise, pleading with, thanking, and talking to God. When you pray for your enemies this way, it changes you. It changes your heart and gives you peace. It changes things in the unseen world. Do you realize that you might be the only person who has ever prayed for the people who are your enemies?

"For our struggle is not against flesh and blood, but against the rulers, against the authorities, against the powers of this dark world and against the spiritual forces of evil in the heavenly realms" (Ephesians 6:12).

Praying, loving, and telling God to "go get 'em" is powerful. It changes you and changes things in the unseen world. You become unbuckled from hate and hugged by love. This is a powerful, life-changing miracle! Love conquers all.

REFLECTION

God hates sin more than we do. Do you pray for your enemies? If so, how do you think this changes things in the unseen world?

PRAYER

Father, thank You that through Your love, "Go get 'em" means rescue them, comfort them, and love them! In fact, let them know Your love so much that they overflow with the beauty and comfort of the Lord. Let them lack no good thing. Let them become everything You created them to be. Remove all evil, all sin, and anything that blocks them from knowing Your peace, understanding, and love. Bless them beyond measure. Comfort them and be their best friend. Let them hear the words "Well done, good and faithful servant." You are in charge! Go get 'em, Lord, go get 'em! Hallelujah! Amen!

Robots versus Free Will

> So, God created mankind in His own image, in the image of God He created them; male and female, He created them.
> —Genesis 1:27

> Then the Lord God formed man of dust from the ground and breathed into his nostrils the breath of life; and man became a living being.
> —Genesis 2:7 (NASB)

Do we really have a choice about anything? And if so, why? Wouldn't it have been a lot easier if God hadn't given us a choice? Then we would never have been hurt or hurt others. There would be no sadness. Anger would not exist. Sin would not exist. If we didn't have a choice, then we would always obey, like robots. On some days I wish I were more like a robot. Every once in a while, I wish my kids were more like robots. We'd all do everything perfectly. We'd look good, act nice, stay in line: no problems here. Life would just be easier, and easy would be so great.

I had a conversation with God about robots versus free will: "Did You struggle with that, God, when You made humans? Probably not. If we all just obeyed You, did everything You said, and were perfect, what would be the purpose in that? You could have just made robots. You, God, are after something deeper: *relationship*. In Psalm 139:13 it says, 'For You created my inmost being; You knit me together in my mother's womb.'

Then You made us valuable and real by giving us a choice. You made us real and precious. Not only that, but it was also Your very breath that breathed life into us! This choice You gave us, of whether we wanted to obey and love You, cost You dearly: a sacrifice of life. Because You gave us free will and choices, Your Son had to die on the cross to restore the relationship because of our bad choices. You made us in the image of God. I'm not sure we can even comprehend what a mighty blessing it is to be made in Your image. I sure am glad You didn't make us in the image of robots. You could have just made us love You, obey You, and cuddle up without question like a good and faithful robotic dog. God, forgive us, because unfortunately, I think we humans try to robot each other. We wish we could program everyone with our rules and systems that we think will make our lives easier. Creating dumb rules and systems seems to be mortals' favorite pastime. We just love standardized testing, growth charts, clothing, style choices, and expectations. Shame on us! We could have much more fun and joy if we didn't do the robot thing to each other. Deep down, each of us gags at the systems and rules that are man-made. God, You didn't make us into robots, so we should not try to make each other into robots. God, thank You for the choice presented in this verse:

"'And the Lord God commanded the man, "You are free to eat from any tree in the garden; but you must not eat from the tree of knowledge of good and evil, for when you eat from it you will certainly die"' (Genesis 2:16–17).

God, thank You for the invitation:

"'Behold, I stand at the door and knock. If anyone hears my voice and opens the door, I will come into him and eat with him, and he with Me' (Revelation 3:20)."

We have a choice with an engraved personal redemptive invitation called *free will*. I am so overwhelmingly thankful that God did not make me, you, or our children into robots. The mess is great. The mess is real. The mess is love!

REFLECTION

What are you angry about?

If free will opened the door for sin to be in the world, how do you handle your sin and others' sin?

Are you thankful or saddened for free will and all that free will causes?

Be honest. Do you prefer to live and force your man-made robotic ways on yourself and others?

PRAYER

Thank You, God, so much that we are a messy, loving bunch of humans made in the image of God. Thank You for the genuine relationship. Thank You for the mess, the love, the forgiveness, and the grace. Thank You for free will. Thank You for the choice, and thank You for forgiving us when we sin. Lord, help me love You and obey You. God, let me give others in my life the same freedom You gave me. Lord, do not let me conform to robot ways. Keep me pure, real, and honest with my anger and questions with You. You can handle all of me. Thank You. Amen.

Casuistry Voices

For by grace you have been saved through faith. And this is not your own doing; it is the gift of God, not a result of works, so that no one may boast.
—Ephesians 2:8–9 (ESV)

No one can know a person's thoughts except that person's own spirit, and no one can know God's thoughts except God's own Spirit.
—1 Corinthians 2:11 (NLT)

Mercy triumphs over judgment, but sometimes I just feel judged and my loved ones feel judged. I'm angry, and I can't get past the ugliness. Help me, Lord! Lord, why do Christians hurt each other so much, when all You do is offer grace, mercy, and love? Er, I'm angry.

The kindest thing you can do for someone is to let them know they matter. You can do this by saying hi, getting to know them, and showing that you care. This is the love of Christ. Judging, wondering, and talking about someone's eternal destination in a mean tone is not showing love. So many times, people have asked me in gossipy tones, "Do you think he or she is a Christian?" or stated, "I don't think they are a Christian." I hate that! It's almost as if they asked in a nasty whisper, "Do you think they have red blood?" Stay away from me. Instead of asking a human about someone else's relationship with God, pray for the person and ask God how He wants you to handle this relationship. After that, ask your friend you were talking with how the two of you can show the love of Christ to the person.

We are not God. You could look at any of us in our lives after we became Christians and think we were definitely not Christians. We are, however, human! Guess what? Humans sin, especially Christians. Has the person asking in that gossipy tone of voice ever truly thought about why he or she asks that question? If you are a Christ follower and you love the Lord with all your heart, mind, and soul, you should never have to ask that question in a mean, gossipy tone or make your judgments about someone else's relationship with God. You should know that God makes every single one of us in His image. We are children of God whom Jesus loves so much that He came to earth and died for all of us while we were still sinners (Romans 5:8). Did you hear that? While you were a sinner, Christ died for you. You. Me. The person you're gossiping about.

You should treat everyone with dignity, respect, and kindness and know that you need to love people and be so kind that they find you emotionally attractive. You should pray for them. Smile at them. Give them grace and mercy. Show them love. Talk to them instead of talking about them! Ask how they are doing. They are children of God whether or not they know Him. Not yours to talk about or whisper about in a nasty judgmental tone of voice. Christ died so we could have a relationship with Him. All our supposed good deeds are like menstrual rags to Him. That sure puts it in perspective, doesn't it?

Be very grateful if you know and love the Lord and have accepted Christ in your heart. It is a gift, opened and accepted by you when you ask Jesus into your heart. Love others. Bless them. Let them be happy that they know you. Be kind, and eventually, once you have become friends with someone, introduce them to Your friend Jesus.

REFLECTION

If Jesus were here today in person walking around with us, would He find your company and your judgments of people attractive?

Would He be angry or pleased with you because of how you treat His loved ones?

Do you need to repent, forgive or be forgiven for 'casuistry voices' in your life? (or all the above-like me)

PRAYER

Lord, let us be so in love with You that we radiate Your love to others. Help us see others the way You see them. Let Your love shine through us so much that we attract others to You. Get us out of the way. You take over. Let us truly love others the way You love us. In Jesus's name. Amen.

Blind or Seeing?

> He replied, "Whether he is a sinner or not, I don't know. One thing I do know. I was blind but now I see!"
> —John 9:25

Mean people make me angry. Mean, arrogant Christians are just so unnecessary. Before you read this, please know that I know there are wonderful churches and beautiful Christians. There are places filled with people where the love of God is so strong that you are in God's sanctuary surrounded by His saints. You can feel the Holy Spirit and the love of Christ in that church. There are also some very evil places and people who disguise themselves using the name of a church and who hide in religion. Churches are not always safe places! Be smart! Very evil people can hide in Christianity. Some even make a living doing this. We need to call them out and not let them ruin the reputations of God-fearing churches and God-fearing Christians.

If you read the books of Matthew, Mark, Luke, and John in the Bible, you will see how much Jesus did not like the religious groups. He disdained the Pharisees, who were constantly trying to trap Him by asking Him baiting questions or questions to get Him in trouble. Jesus healed on the Sabbath multiple times. It infuriated the religious leaders because He was breaking the law that one should not work on the Sabbath. What is so disdainful about a Pharisee is that they think they are an example to others, a godly example, *an untouchable example.* God just calls His people to be real and love Him with all their hearts, minds, and souls.

Stop, reflect, and ask yourself, "Is this me?"

When you are so arrogant that you think you are an example of godliness, it can get scarily evil. You now feel you need to hide and cover up your struggle. You need to show your power and protect your status. The very one you were opposed to at the beginning—the devil—now has your ear and eventually has your heart. Your only defense is to be humble and cry out from the bottom of your soul, "I can't do this. I fail. I struggle. I need Jesus. We all need Jesus."

The Pharisees were there to protect the rules and their jobs! Two thousand years later, not much has changed, and this spirit remains. Jesus was there to teach them that being healed was more important than following the rules. He healed the man in question on the Sabbath *because He loved him*. It is so easy to slip into being mean, to think about the rules, the systems, your reputation, and the programs that you believe are more important than the people. You see it all the time in organizations and people who go caustic. If something is done that is unorthodox according to the people in charge, they feel threatened and imposed upon with their feathers in a ruffle. They puff up and defend their territory. They might have started their journey with passion and love, but somewhere along the way they lost their joy and now just want to protect their little sandcastles that they take credit for building—or just cruise into retirement. They traded their passion for a paycheck and pompous power. Walk away from these folks. When programs, reputations, and status become more important than people, it's a slippery slope!

Again, stop and ask, "Is this me? Have I done this?" (I have and deeply regret it.)

This is where the rubber meets the road. You know better. You can see yourself outside your body telling you to stop. You feel the Holy Spirit warning you, *Don't say it. Don't do it. Walk away. Loosen up. People are more important than your agenda and reputation.* It is one thing to sin because you don't know better. It is a whole other thing to sin when you know better. It's a slippery, evil slope.

REFLECTION

Have you ever felt that you should be an "example" of what a Christian should look like? If so, does this make you feel that you can't share your pain, sins, and struggles? Why?

Do you like fake people who pretend to be perfect? Are you fake sometimes?

Figuratively, are you blind or can you see?

Who do you need to humbly apologize to?

Is there someone you need to protect? Do you need to confront someone?

PRAYER

Lord, heal our hearts when we have been hurt by mean people. Heal those we have hurt because we were being mean people. Lord, open the eyes of our hearts and give us true wisdom. Let us celebrate when people come to Jesus! Lord, don't let us be a part of the fake religious cliques and meanness. Keep us open to You. Protect our hearts. Make us real. Help us to be vulnerable. Take away judgment of others. Lord, take away evil. Let us truly see people through the love of Christ. Let us love and bless Your creation! Keep us raw honest. Amen.

Huge Gap

> For God so loved the world that He gave His one and only Son, that whoever believes in Him should not perish but have eternal life.
> —John 3:16

In my anger and hurt, I find a huge gap that brings me to my knees in prayer and then causes me to worship because of how much God loves me. There is a vast gap separating us from God. Many times, we humans try to swing over the gap with a flimsy rope, when there is a beautiful bridge shaped like a cross closing the gap right in front of us. We swing back and forth over this gap with good intentions and righteous acts, when all we need to do is use the cross Jesus died on to close the gap.

The problem with us humans is that we live in human bodies, and because of this we mess up. So, I ask you to know that Christians are human just like you. Often, they hurt each other so badly that they do the devil's work for him. The church in its purest form is just a bunch of hypocritical sinners who are so desperate for Christ that they realize they need to get together even with messy sin all over them and proclaim they love and need Christ. If Christians don't try to attain all that God asks of us, then we are pathetic and just living small, selfish, ordinary lives. Christians are supposed to continue to try, and fail, try and fail, but always keep trying. Our goal is to be like Christ. It's impossible, but in those pure moments when we are living through Christ, we experience a love so great that we know it's worth trying. Grace, mercy, forgiveness, and love help us on our way. We can't get there on our own. We need God. It is as if we just aren't home here on earth and know we are just passing through and that our eventual destination is gonna be good.

If you don't know where you are going, you will end up nowhere or someplace worse. Christians know where we want to be but just can't do it on our own. When we die, the long struggle will be over. It is a battle! We are constantly struggling with our selfish sin and asking God to take over. It's really a simple faith; we try but know we can't do it on our own. God rescues us, forgives us, and gives us strength, and we just keep going, knowing we can only do this thing called life through Christ's love. We also struggle with the image of what a Christian should look like and the fact that we rarely look or act that way. Sometimes we try to pretend we are perfect, and that does even more damage because we know we aren't.

There will always be a tremendous gap until Jesus comes back or we walk across that bridge into God's arms. Christians constantly must confess, repent, and let Jesus fill that gap again and again. If we could fill the gap with wonderful works or sheer might, we would, and then we would be proud and arrogant! The good news is that only Jesus fills the gap. It is a good, humbling thing to know this.

REFLECTION

How do you describe Christians?

In a way, the very word *Christian* is confusing: someone who has been saved by Jesus yet still messes up and hurts others; someone who loves Christ and should love others but constantly falls short and messes up, yet is still forgiven; a loved, forgiven, and sinful hypocrite.

Does this definition make you detest Christians or cause you to know you, too, are welcome?

PRAYER

Lord, I can't wait to be in heaven when the long struggle is over. Keep me humble, confessing and realizing I can only do life well through You. Let nothing separate me from You. You are my all. Live through me. Love others through me. Amen

Epiphany

> But if Christ is in you, then even though your body is subject to death because of sin, the Spirit gives life because of righteousness. And if the Spirit of Him who raised Jesus from the dead is living in you, He who raised Christ from the dead will also give life to your mortal bodies because of His Spirit who lives in you. Therefore, brothers and sisters, we have an obligation—but it is not to the flesh, to live according to it. For if you live according to the flesh you will die; but if by the Spirit you put to death the misdeeds of the body, you will live. For those who are led by the Spirit of God are the children of God. The Spirit you received does not make you slaves, so that you live in fear again; rather, the Spirit you received brought about your adoption to sonship. And by Him we cry, "Abba, Father."
> —Romans 8:10–15

In your anger, you often realize that you are angry at yourself. This is part of the healing.

I had an epiphany: there is so much ugly sin in me. Bumping straight into myself made me not very happy. I saw myself for what I was, and I was not impressed. Pampered, spoiled, and directing life according to my own wishes, well, it was ugly.

I thought I knew You, God. I thought I was for You, God. I thought I had given You all. There is so much ugly sin in me. I am full of pride. I'm judgmental, stubborn, dumb, and mean. I'm self-centered. I want things only my way, and I want only what I think is best. I haven't loved like I should; I have been cruel and have thought myself better than others. I have been thoughtless and selfish. I thought I had given You my all. But I had not. I thought things were supposed to go a certain way: that I wouldn't get sick, mess up, and sin. I nailed You to the cross with my ugly ways. I thought I was a great mom. I think it was just because things were going great. Do I only love when others are lovable and when life is good? I had an epiphany: I need God very badly. I can't even breathe without Him.

Take me. Change me. All of me. I am worthless and need You, God.

Take over. Redeem me. Make me Yours, God. Make me like me. I want You in charge.

REFLECTION

Are you angry at yourself? If so, for what? Do you know that you are forgiven? Can you let yourself be forgiven?

PRAYER

Lord, I don't like the sin in me. I don't like who I have become. There is ugliness all over me. Take it away. Forgive me. In Jesus's name, I declare: I only live through Christ now. All fleshly sinful ways of the world are dead in me. The spirit of Christ lives in me. The rest of me is dead. I am blessed with life and peace, and my spirit is alive because of Christ's righteousness. My mortal body has life through the Holy Spirit. I have the spirit of sonship. Abba, Father! I am God's child. I cling to You, Jesus. You are in charge, not me. Thank You for that, God. Amen.

Let's Celebrate

> Meanwhile, the older son was in the field. When he came near the house, he heard music and dancing. So, he called one of the servants and asked him what was going on. "Your brother has come," he replied, "and your father has killed the fattened calf because he has him back safe and sound." The older brother became angry and refused to go in. So, his father went out and pleaded with him. But he answered his father, "Look! All these years I've been slaving for you and never disobeyed your orders. Yet you never gave me even a young goat so I could celebrate with my friends. But when this son of yours who has squandered your property with prostitutes comes home, you kill the fattened calf for him!" "My son," the father said, "you are always with me, and everything I have is yours. But we had to celebrate and be glad, because this brother of yours was dead and is alive again; he was lost and is found."
> —Luke 15:25–31

If you can't party, especially at someone else's celebration, then this is a sure sign that you are still ugly angry about something. It could be a childhood experience you have buried; it could be unforgiveness; it could be that you think the world owes you something. Life is not fair, so when it is time to celebrate, you choose to pout and be sour.

Are you able to party and celebrate those who are rescued, forgiven, and redeemed by Christ, or do you just cross your arms and grumble that they have gotten away with so much? In the parable of the lost prodigal, the older son just can't celebrate the return of his brother. It says so much about the condition of his heart. When you can't celebrate the turnaround of a lost soul and don't like to hear their testimonies, what does this say about you? Is it saying, "I have worked my bum off, I have been faithful, and I sure would like a party celebrating me"? "Hello? What about me?" The father is very kind in his response. It shows the condition of his heart too. He tells his oldest son that everything he has belongs to the oldest son and that he should already know this in his heart. That there is the problem. Don't we know that all Jesus has is ours? He doesn't run out of favor, love, healing, success, joy, money, or laughter. If you truly believe that everything in heaven and earth belongs to God, then why would you ever cross your arms and stay outside when someone comes back to Jesus? Why would you remind someone of where they have been and what they have gone through in a judgmental tone? Don't you think they know that? If you can't party when a caterpillar becomes a butterfly and when one of God's children is saved, then you should take some dancing lessons.

If we truly know the love, forgiveness, and joy of Christ, then we are the very first to set up the party when one of God's children finds their way home to Him.

REFLECTION

Do you celebrate others well, or are you most often suspicious, angry, and jealous?

PRAYER

Lord, everything in heaven and on earth belongs to You. You never run out of favor, love, healing, forgiveness, or resources. You are my Father. I rest in You. I trust in You. In Jesus's name, I declare: I celebrate when Your children come home to You. I celebrate others. I dance and party with You and them. You are amazing. Thank You for Your blessings! Amen.

Surrender

> I have been crucified with Christ and I no longer live, but Christ lives in me. The life I now live in the body, I live by faith in the Son of God, who loved me and gave Himself for me.
> —Galatians 2:20

If you are not ready to party, then you are probably not ready to surrender. Go back into your past and visit those hard places and face what hurt you and makes you angry. Make it real. When you're done, at the end of being angry, you will run into surrender. The question is, though, what do you want to surrender to? If you want to surrender to anger and misery, then go to the dump. If you want to surrender to a life worth living, then forgive. If you are really hurting, you might choose to go to visit the dump and exit through forgiveness. Whatever you do, please, please don't stay in the dump. It's not a good place. Not at all. Complete surrender to God is what makes life wonderful and worth living. It's scary to let go, but it's worth it!

What prevents us from completely surrendering to God? Fear, bad memories, betrayal by those who claim to know Christ, lack of trust, not wanting to let go, arrogance, a hard heart, anger, bitterness, the lies of the enemy, busyness, disappointment, feeling that God wasn't there for us, rejection, sin, loving our way more than God's way, wanting to be in control, lacking in faith. The list can go on and on and include things more personal than what I have mentioned. I think for me it is not realizing how much God loves me, a lack of trusting Him, and being afraid of more pain and hardships. If I totally understand how much God loves me, then I have nothing to fear.

The love that God has for us is not a faraway love or a distant love that allows us to bother Him only for the big stuff. The love God has for us is intimate. He cares about every single detail of our lives. It will take more than a lifetime to understand this. He formed the earth, and everything in heaven and earth belongs to Him, yet He knows every detail of life. He knit us together with loving care. He knows every breath we take. He knows what we need before we even ask Him. He is in the details. Totally surrendering to Him means going to the Creator and asking Him to take over. "Lord, make me everything You created me to be." Let's stop tripping and falling over our desires, pain, and bad memories.

What do you have to fear, pain? Pain can be a gift. It can chisel away of what you do not need, such as lies, bad habits, arrogance, bad memories, manipulation, unforgiveness, and sin.

If we really trust God and know that He loves us and the ones we love, then even when His answer is pain and hardship, we can trust that this is best for us. He is refining us and taking away things and lies we don't need. Pain and heartbreak are miserable, but true misery is a life not surrendered to God. I know that Jeremiah 29:11 is true: "'For I know the plans I have for you,' declares the Lord, 'plans to prosper you and not to harm you, plans to give you hope and a future.'"

If God is prospering us through pain or hardships, then we can thank Him and trust Him. Life on earth is short. How sad to get to the end of our days and realize we missed the adventure of our only lifetime because we sought to avoid pain or hardship.

REFLECTION

What do you want to surrender to?

Is there anything blocking you from knowing that God loves you?

Would you be willing to ask God to remove what is blocking you from the love of Christ?

PRAYER

Jesus, I don't want to live in pain, regret and anger anymore. I really don't. Untangle me from anger and pain. I declare this instead: Lord, I have been crucified with Christ, and I no longer live, but You live in me. The life I now live in the body, I live by faith in the Son of God, who loved me and gave Himself for me. I belong to You. Amen.

Faith

> Now faith is confidence in what we hope for and assurance about what we do not see.
> —Hebrews 11:1

Do we surrender to a faith we can't completely know or experience this side of heaven, or do we just lick our wounds and stay angry? Faith is a good choice. Hebrews 11:1 is my absolute favorite verse. It has helped me get through some dark times. I have prayed for what I cannot see as if it has already happened. I have thanked God for prayers He hasn't answered as if He has answered them. This verse has seen me through to the other side. It helps me cling to Christ and pray scriptures in the Bible. God must chuckle at me. I will start my prayers to Him with thanks and remind Him I am praying Hebrews 11:1 style. I thank God for the prayers He will answer in my future.

Faith. What is faith? The definition is "complete trust or confidence in someone or something." What does *sure* mean? To be sure is to have confidence in what one thinks or knows, having no doubt that one is right. What is hope? Hope is a feeling of expectation and a desire for a certain thing to happen. Faith is sure of what we hope for. What do we hope for? We can hope for a lot of things. We can pray for a lot of things. The group known as "Moms in Prayer" teaches us to pray Bible verses for your kids. When we are praying Bible verses, we know that we are praying God's will.

We can hope for things that are not God's will. My prayers for myself and others are to let my desires be God's desires and to let God's desires be my desires. I ask that He let me line up with His will.

How do we know God's desires? He left us a love letter in the Bible. He left us stories, adventures, wisdom, and guidance. Read it. Pray it. Ask for fresh eyes and for your heart to be open. Faith is what we hope for and entails being certain of what we do not see. From my perspective, I think "certain of what we do not see" means we should go ahead and thank God for prayers He hasn't answered yet, as if He has already answered them. If hope is an expectation and desire for a certain thing to happen, and if I am praying scripture and God's will, I am comfortable going ahead and thanking Him for what I believe is going to happen. It's like talking about my hopes and dreams with my spouse and then making them happen. Hebrews 11:1 discusses a faith that is planning for God to hear me: praying God's will and scripture and thanking Him for His will to be done. God is that sweet, kind, and intimate.

Plan on it. Pray for it. Praise and thank God for it before it happens. Then *trust*. He hears you. He is a good Father and will do what is best.

Prayer makes a difference, Hebrews 11:1 style and all.

REFLECTION

Are you willing to let go of anger and allow faith and hope to take over?

PRAYER

Lord, increase my faith. Take away my anger at You and myself. Help me stop licking my wounds. Let me get the focus off my anger and pain and see Your love. I'm going to focus on You. I thank You for the Bible. I thank You for scripture. I thank You for faith. Many times, I don't know how to pray, and I am thankful for Your Word, which teaches me how to pray. Give me scripture to pray and hold on to. Thank You for direction, guidance, and prayer. Amen.

Hope

> "For I know the plans that I have for you," declares the Lord, "plans to prosper you and not to harm you, plans to give you hope and a future."
> —Jeremiah 29:11

Do we dare to leave our anger and begin to have hope again? Without hope, life is hopeless. All anyone needs is a little hope to keep going. Hope feeds us, encourages us, and cheers us to get past the finish line. We all have seen someone who has given up. They have no hope. It almost feels that the dark side has stolen their very being. We need to give them a jug of hope and introduce them to the One who gives hope. The interesting thing about hope is that it is always hungry. It is like a hole in us that keeps asking for more. This hole can only be filled by our Creator. He is the ultimate hope answer.

Hope is a popular word among high school and college students in Georgia. The state of Georgia has the Hope Scholarship for high school graduates. It gives hope. It's a fantastic deal. Do great in school, take the right classes, and you can get a great deal of college paid for, funded by people who *hope* they can win the lottery. Therefore, many people are moving to Georgia. *Hope* is a noble word to describe this scholarship. Why does it work? The lottery funds it. We all have an innate desire for hope. We hope we can win the lottery. Every lottery ticket sold is a little hope gamble that we can beat the odds. The odds are so low to win that it is funny. According to CNBC, the chances of winning the $1 billion Mega Millions in October 2017 were 1 in 302.6 million. Still, what is the fun thing to do when the lottery prize gets high? Talk about what you would do with the money and then buy lottery tickets. Honestly, I never want to win. I think it would ruin me unless I were so self-controlled that I could give most of the money away. Good old-fashioned saving your pennies and dimes is the way to go. You appreciate it more. However, if you are a graduating Georgia high school student, the Hope Scholarship is a great deal. That is why I don't mind every once in a while buying a lottery ticket. It gives hope to the students of Georgia. They can work and study hard and get much of college or tech school paid for. The

Hope Scholarship is dangled out there for our Georgia students. It offers hope and a hope standard.

Hope is a beautiful thing; without hope, life is hopeless. However, hope is always hungry; it is a hole that keeps asking for more. We will always need hope for all the days of our lives. Each one of us has a hope hole in our being. We can fill it with dreams, stuff, busyness, success, money, drugs, sex, etc.—use your imagination. We keep hoping to fill that hole with anything that will help us and make us feel better. Jesus is the only One who can fill the hope hole in our being.

Jesus is our winning ticket, and the splendid news is that He is not a lottery. The Holy Spirit is here to fill that hole in our being and wants each one of us to be the ultimate winner of an abundant hope-filled life with Jesus.

REFLECTION

Do you feel hopeless? Do you like that feeling?

Do you think you have an empty hole in the center of you that always needs filling?

What do you think would finally satisfy that empty hole in you?

PRAYER

God, Jesus, and the Holy Spirit, You are my hope. Help me to see You. Fill my life with You. I thank You for that empty hole in me that can only be filled by You. I know that the plans You have for me are to prosper me and give me hope and a future. Your plans are best. I can trust You. Amen.

By Faith

> Now faith is confidence in what we hope for and assurance about what we do not see.
> —Hebrews 11:1

Choose faith. Leave the anger behind. Have you ever heard someone say, "If I had known what I was getting into or what I was going to go through, I would have never done it"? That is the gift. We don't know. We live by faith.

Sometimes you just must take a step of faith and go for it, not knowing what will happen or where you will end up. If you knew, you would probably play it safe and live in your little hobbit hole forever.

There is a mighty adventure out there for us, one full of dragons, castles, mighty battles, love, heartbreak, and life. Go for it. Take that first step and walk out the door. In Hebrews 11, every mighty description of the noble patriarchs' life history starts with "By faith." Let's not be any different. By faith, ask the girl out; say yes; call someone; reach out; be social; apologize; change jobs; do what your heart desires even if no one understands (where would we be without Disney World or Snoopy?) tell the truth; stick up for someone; forgive; give an epic grace bomb; stop feeling sorry for yourself; run the marathon; give generously; start the company; say "I love you"; get married; have children; go on the first date; even if rejected get back up and try again and again and again; when necessary don't take no for an answer; go to church; go back to church; read your Bible; find out if God really exists; put yourself out there.

You only get one life! Live it! Get out there and find your adventure!

REFLECTION

Working through anger is healthy. Staying angry and mad at God, the world, and yourself isn't healthy. Since you only get one life, do you really want to just be angry, or do you want to live by faith?

Read John 8:11. How can you apply this verse to your life?

PRAYER

Lord, by faith we trust You. By faith, we let go of anger and hurt. By faith, we pray verses in the Bible. By faith, we love others. By faith, we forgive others. By faith, we hope. By faith, we go for it. By faith, we see things that cannot be seen yet. By faith, we take that first step while holding on to Your promises. By faith, *we live*. Amen.

CONCLUSION OF SECTION VI

Being angry is exhausting. It takes a lot out of you. It is okay to be angry about an evil injustice, a disappointment, sin, death, or tragedy. Life is not fair. Life is foul sometimes. If we don't admit that anger exists, and if we are disappointed with the sin we are surrounded by on earth, then we don't really know God.

Sin makes God angry too, so much so that He can't be around it. What God did is unthinkable. He canceled sin. He canceled the authority of sin through His only Son's death on the cross. This truth needs to sink into your soul. This truth can scrape the ugliness off your heart.

Sometimes this happens when you rest. You give being angry, hurt, sad, and devastated a break. You go get some rest and gain some perspective.

Section VII

REST

Rest well before you decide where you will take your next step: at the dump or on the hard road to forgiveness. A rest will give you the right perspective.

> Rest, My sweet one, rest. Hop up on My lap and get some rest. I'll cuddle you while you rest and tell you your hair count today.

O you are so tired of it all. Worn out. You need help. You need rest. You need a break from the anger, hurt, misunderstandings, and difficulties.

Sometimes we are lucky enough to get to change the scenery and go on a vacation. Other times we must make our own vacations: a long walk, a soak in the bathtub, kayaking, going out to lunch with a friend, giving ourselves permission to snuggle with the dog on the couch when a dirty house stares back at us. Give yourself time to renew yourself. Take care of you.

On the following pages you will find devotions to help you rest and renew.

My Peter Pan Trip

> And He said: "Truly I tell you, unless you change and become like little children, you will never enter the kingdom of heaven."
> —Matthew 18:3

You can go on a Peter Pan trip anytime in your mind. Give yourself permission to be young in your heart again and hang out with the Lost Boys. If I could go back and slap my young mom self around and say, "Get yourself together and don't take this whole thing so seriously," I would slap myself hard into some perspective. Life goes by too quickly not to enjoy it. The above verse tells us to become like little children, or else we won't enter the kingdom of heaven. It took me awhile, but I joined up with the Lost Boys and learned to play again.

It is good that Paul in the Bible never tells us what his thorn in his flesh is. It would have been too easy for us to dismiss it and say, "Well, I would never do that or struggle with that issue," be our mean selves. It would have been too easy for my former self to say, "Well, I would never have to deal with that."

So, my slap-worn-out self went on my twenty-fifth anniversary trip with my sweet husband. We made some rules. No talking about woes and no talking about jobs. We had a blast! We stayed in the same cottage we had stayed in on our honeymoon. So much fun. I realized once again why we had fallen in love. I could focus on what was important and realized that kids should not be put above our marriage and the relationship with my husband. I am guilty of that but have repented. Then my husband totally surprised me on my fiftieth birthday by having my sister and her husband show up on our vacation. Oh my goodness, it was the best present ever! Our rule: don't talk about woes or jobs. About the third day in, I remembered a quote from the movie *Hook* when Peter Pan returns as an adult to Neverland and the only way to save his kids is to become a kid himself again so he can fly and thus save his kids. Peter as an adult had become like a pirate. Bad! I am afraid we all become like pirates if we take ourselves and life too seriously. Once Peter learns to fly and use his imagination again, Tinker Bell has to slap him around and remind him he is in Neverland to save his kids. Peter looks at Tinker Bell and says, "I have kids? What are their names?" Every once in a while we need to get away and have Peter Pan time. We need to be the kids again—relax, play, and take naps, with the hardest decision to make being if we should swim in the ocean or the pool. We need to say, like Peter would, "I have a job? What do I do? I have a mortgage? Where do I live?" It gives us a good perspective and reminds us that unless we become like little children, we cannot enter the gates of heaven. And the thing is, why in the world do we worry about our kids, jobs, money, etc., so much anyway? God has got all of it in His hands. He can do a much better job of protecting and loving us and our loved ones than we can!

I challenge you to join the Lost Boys and go on a Peter Pan trip! Better yet, stay a child at heart! Let awe and wonder surround you.

REFLECTION

When was the last time you played?

Do you allow your children to let you be human (see your faults, respect your needs, see you play)?

PRAYER

Heavenly Father, help us not to take ourselves so seriously. In Philippians 4:6–7 it says, "Do not be anxious about anything, but in everything by prayer and supplication with thanksgiving let your requests be made known to God." Lord, we give You our request. We thank You that nothing is impossible for You. We trust You. Father, let us become like little children and frolic in our trust of You. You are good. Help us to rest and renew. We love You. Amen.

You Know What I'm Saying? No, No I Do Not!

> Two are better than one, because they have a good return for their labor: if either of them falls down, one can help them up. But pity anyone who falls and has no one to help them up. Also, if two lie down together, they will keep warm. But how can one keep warm alone? Though one may be overpowered, two can defend themselves. A cord of three is not quickly broken.
> —Ecclesiastes 4:9–12

Peter Pan had fun because he was with other people. He would have been desperately lonely without other kids to hang out with. We are no different. We need people. We need help. We need to help each other. The best part about having a child's heart is knowing you can't do this thing called life all by yourself. You need friends. Sometimes you need to rest in the knowledge that somebody else is better at helping you and the people you love than you are. Lone wolves are just that: lone wolves. Lonely. You need a wolf pack to thrive. You need some other wolves in your life to help growl and keep the pack in shape. Parents and families who go it alone, well, they are lonely and, quite frankly, a little weird. You need other people to help you and help raise your kids. Grandparents, relatives, friends, coaches, neighbors, other parents, other adults, and teachers all play an important role in developing children into successful, happy adults. We need other people in our lives.

Do you ever get so many emails from one source that you literally don't even look at them anymore? Every day the same information bombards you repeatedly. It becomes extremely frustrating, and even if there is additional information, you are so over it that you don't even read it. I am afraid my kids feel that way about me right now because I have said the same things and drilled the same information into them for so long that they don't even hear me anymore. They hear what Charlie Brown heard when his parents talked to him: "Wong wah ah wahong waw awa." I loved it when my kids were little and they thought I was great. One time when my oldest, Harrison, was at the beach with me (he was about four), he yelled at me because his sandcastle got knocked down by the ocean. Couldn't I stop the waves? Oh, sweetie! If only I were that powerful to command the waves and they would listen. Wow, he really thought I oversaw waves. Ha-ha-ha! I would always still be up when he went to bed and would be up before he awoke. He probably thought I didn't sleep either. Those days were great. Exhausting, but great. It's not a good feeling when your kids realize how sinful you really are: they are firsthand witnesses to your mess-ups! Please don't even mention to me those teenage years when just by existing we embarrass the fool out of them. Don't forget the early twenties when they know everything and are "enlightened" and we are just dumb and out of touch. Did we ever even go to college? Yes, but it was in caveman times. This is when I just must shut up. Put the lock on my mouth and throw away the key. Put it in reverse, woman. The less I say, the better off we all are. My tongue becomes like chewing gum. I pray that someone else will tell them what I want them to hear: "Lord, let there be people in their lives who truly love them, people who have godly wisdom and whose advice my children will respect." Families that go it alone do themselves a great disservice. There is no one else to say what their kids need to hear. You need people to talk to, disciple, and speak the truth to your kids besides you.

If you are trying to go at life alone or parent alone, stop. You need help and you need friends. The more, the better! You need people in your life to say what you want your loved ones to hear and to say what you need to hear. Who cares who gets the credit? Just let us all receive the message one way or another: God loves you, and His plans are to bless you and prosper you! Rest in God's provision of help from others.

REFLECTION

Do you think you are a weak person if you ask people for help?

To have friends is risky, and to have them you must be vulnerable, forgiving, and available. Would you describe yourself as a vulnerable, forgiving, and available person? If not, what steps can you take to change?

How can knowing you can't do it all by yourself help you rest and trust God more?

PRAYER

Holy Father, thank You for all the people who love whom I love. Lord, thank You for the people who invest in my loved ones' lives. Lord, please continue to bring people to disciple me and to love me and my loved ones. In Jesus's name let my loved ones and me love You so much that we also disciple and love others. Let me truly trust in You and, in that trust, find true rest and peace that passes all understanding. Thank You for the people You bring into my life to help me. Amen.

Deliberately Nailed

I am the Good Shepherd; I know My sheep and My sheep know Me—just as the Father knows Me and I know the Father—and I lay down My life for the sheep. I have other sheep that are not of this sheep pen. I must bring them also. They too will listen to My voice, and there shall be one flock and one Shepherd. The reason My Father loves Me is that I lay down my life—only to take it up again. No one takes it from Me, but I lay it down of My own accord. I have authority to lay it down and authority to take it up again. This command I received from My Father.
—John 10:14–17

When we rest and get away, we realize how much God loves us. Rest and a change of pace give us perspective. Perspective reveals to us just how much God loves us. Often, I wonder about the unseen world—angels, demons, and the spiritual struggle that goes on around us. When Jesus willingly died on the cross, an entire heaven full of angels watched and held their breath. The sacrifice that Jesus made by dying on the cross for my sins is hard to comprehend.

As I am going through a fast (not eating delicious food I so badly crave) right now, I am reminded of how Jesus was consciously, deliberately, and willingly nailed to the cross. All He had to do was speak, and a multitude of angels would have delivered Him. He stayed on that cross willingly. Deliberately. My tiny little fast with a multitude of food choices all around me allows me to quietly connect with just a very small fraction of what Christ did for me. He didn't have to die on the cross. He had angels and God to stop it. He chose to follow through. He loved me and you that much. When I don't eat when there are so many yummy foods around me, I am overwhelmed by what Jesus did for me. He chose to die for my sins, to rescue me, to set me free. I think if we could have seen the unseen world of angels surrounding Him, ready to rescue Him at that cross while He bled and gasped for each breath, we ourselves wouldn't be able to catch our breath when confronted with what a deliberate, loving act He did for us. So today, when I see such wonderful food choices in front of me and say no and pray and worship God instead, I can realize a tiny bit more just how much Jesus loves me and you.

"For our struggle is not against flesh and blood, but against the rulers, against the authorities, against the powers of this dark world and against the spiritual forces of evil in the heavenly realms" (Ephesians 6:1).

I'm not sure if I want to see the unseen world; it might scare the fool outta me. It is important, though, to understand what Jesus did for us when He died on that cross for our *sins*!

REFLECTION

Fasting can take many forms: silence, no electronics, no food. It involves giving something up in order to concentrate on God more. Would you be willing to give up something today to help you focus more on God?

PRAYER

Lord, thank You for deliberately dying on the cross for my sins. Thank You that when I take a rest from food, I can see Your sacrifice on the cross a little better. Your love is so great, I barely understand the depth and width of it. Amen.

Real Heroes

> When I was a child, I talked like a child, I thought like a child, I reasoned like a child. When I became a man, I put the ways of childhood behind me.
> —1 Corinthians 3:11

When we truly understand what a real hero is, we can relax, feel love, and love others. Lots of times what gives us angst is not understanding the truth. When we get rid of unrealistic expectations of what life should look like, we are able to truly rest in Christ.

Who is your hero, and why? It's a hard question to answer if you think heroes should be superhuman: Wonder Woman, Batman, the Rescue Heroes, the Power Rangers. Or you can go saintly: Mother Teresa, Mahatma Gandhi, Jesus. When asked that question, don't you want to say a real person is your hero? Wouldn't you like a personable relationship with your hero and really know your hero? When we are young, we want a hero, someone we can believe in and who will set the right example for us. People often ask younger children, "Who is your hero?" It is such a weird question. I never really knew how to answer that question when asked. It is easier if the person is a superhero or made up because eventually actual humans disappoint us. It is part of being human. I could not answer the question because my standard for a hero was childish. An authentic hero is someone who loves, messes up, asks for forgiveness, laughs, hugs, is humble, and lets God direct his or her life.

Let's put our childish ways behind us and realize that the best heroes are humans who love, forgive, love, forgive, ask for forgiveness, and love some more. They are overcomers, complete surrender to God kind of people. Real heroes are bathed in grace, humbleness, and mercy. They are beautiful souls who belong to God. It's messy down here in these earthly realms, but it is not impossible to live for the Lord, cling to the cross, and live life like a hero.

"When I was a child, I talked like a child, I thought like a child, I reasoned like a child. When I became a man, I put the ways of childhood behind me" (1 Corinthians 3:11).

An authentic hero is someone who can apologize, forgive, be forgiven, love, and allow God to be in charge and redeem any situation. Let's rest in the real definition of a hero and give the people around us the freedom to be real.

REFLECTION

Do you allow the people (parents, children, friends, bosses, ministers) in your life to be human (mess up, be forgiven, forgive)? Why or why not?

Define what you think a real hero is.

Do your expectations of yourself and others change when you allow grace into the picture? How can this help you rest in the love and mercy of Christ?

PRAYER

Lord, let us be Your superheroes full of love, forgiveness, humility and complete surrender to You. Nothing is impossible for You, God (Luke 1:37). We rest in Your love and mercy. We forgive and we are forgiven. We have grace and we give grace. We are loved and we love. Amen.

Take It Personally

> Do you not know that you are God's temple and that God's Spirit dwells in you?
> —1 Corinthians 3:10–12 (ESV)

When I am tired and frustrated, I often want to eat. I should rest, but instead I eat food that isn't good for me but offers a temporary, happy, sugar-induced high. What I really need is rest and perspective, not chocolate. Take it personally, because when you feel tired and hopeless, you often just don't want to take care of yourself. It feels good to punish your body by drinking, overeating, and getting fat. It is a temporary satisfaction to relieve your stress, but it only causes more stress.

It is very important to take care of the bodies that house us. We honor God by honoring ourselves and taking care of our bodies. When I am upset, I either exercise or eat. Exercise is a good outlet. Eating is not. I know better, but it just feels good sometimes to sulk over a big helping of ganache cake and ice cream. The problem with this is that it is not good for me at all. I can't get away from myself and the body I'm trapped in.

Your body is a temple. You are sacred. Your body is sacred. You need to take care of yourself. Exercise, eat healthy, rest, forgive, be nice to yourself, groom yourself, take your necessary medicine and vitamins, take care of your teeth, and go to the doctor and dentist. Be the best you can be. You are stuck in this body for as long as you live. Don't destroy your temple. Don't let others destroy your temple. Be extremely picky about whom you marry and whom you associate with. You are sacred! Take it personally!

We need to take care of ourselves. We need to protect ourselves from bad habits, dangerous substances, and people who want to harm us. We need to rest and trust in Christ.

REFLECTION

How can you be selfishly unselfish by taking care of yourself?

How will this make you behave better to the people around you?

PRAYER

Lord, let me take care of my body and Your temple. Help me to eat healthy food, get enough rest, and exercise. Protect me from unhealthy relationships. Bring me God-fearing friends. Lord, make me Yours on the inside and out. Let me be beautiful on the inside and out. May I rest in You. Amen.

Honesty

> He took the blind man by the hand and led him outside the village. When He had spit on the man's eyes and put His hands on him, Jesus asked, "Do you see anything?" He looked up and said, "I see people; they look like trees walking around." Once more Jesus put His hands on the man's eyes. Then his eyes were opened, his sight was restored, and he saw everything clearly.
> —Mark 8:23–25

When we are tired and worn out and life has beaten us down, sometimes we need a big spoonful of honesty and then a slap on the heinie that tells us not to settle for being less than! The difference between being honest and being dishonest is like the difference between people looking like trees and your sight being perfect. Honesty with yourself, God, and others makes you see clearly. Sometimes I make life fuzzy because I just want to settle with the beginning of a miracle. I'm exhausted, don't want to pray or fast anymore, or just want to take the easy way out. "Yeah, it's good enough. It's better than it was. I can be satisfied with this." This story about the blind man seeing trees that look like people has always been a little confusing to me until recently.

The Bible speaks to me many times. The above verse just came alive to me. I've read it many times, but tonight I was the blind man, and when I was the blind man, I settled for people looking like trees because I didn't want to be rude or hurt anyone's feelings and because I was tired. This made me examine myself and my relationships. Why am I doing this? I would not have wanted to have hurt Jesus's feelings and would have just been content with people looking like trees. Wow, how silly and dumb is that! Jesus knew that the man saw people looking like trees! I think Jesus just wanted the man to be honest. God wants me to be honest too. As I wrestled with this verse, I thought about all the ways I have settled for "satisfied" in situations because that is easiest for me in relationships and in my prayers. Peace is great; conflicts, not so much! So, I had a talk with God. I confessed and asked for forgiveness for the times when I have settled in my heart and relationships for "people looking like trees." It was as if I picked up the pile of half-answered prayers and partially fulfilled dreams and decided to be honest about it with myself and God.

Honesty with yourself, God, and others allows you to see clearly. Only when you are honest can you truly rest and renew.

REFLECTION

Are there areas in your life where you have settled for less than God's best? List them.

PRAYER

Lord, I remember the story in the Bible where Jesus was sound asleep in a boat during a wicked storm. The disciples were panicked. They thought they were going to die. Jesus, You were so tired. You chose to rest. You know what it is like to be utterly exhausted. Thank You for the visual of resting during a storm. Even when life is hard and exhausting, You can provide us rest and peace that passes all understanding. Give us your peace that passes all understanding. Take our burdens, Lord, and give us hope. Breathe on us. You don't want us to exist being satisfied when prayers or life is not all it should be, not Your best plan. We don't want to be satisfied when "people still look like trees." Keep me honest with You and with others. Don't let me live to please people, but let me live to please You. Keep me faithful in my prayers and relationships, even when it is uncomfortable. Thank You, Lord. Amen.

One Good Decision Away

> A sluggard's appetite is never filled, but the desires of the diligent are fully satisfied.
> —Proverbs 13:4

Should you be brave? Should you get up out of the bed and celebrate a new day? It is so hard to be brave rather than tired and scared. This is because we tend to look at the entire lifetime, which illuminates how hard it will be to take this next step. When you are tired, you can become a little scared, like a frightened animal not wanting to leave the safety of the nest. Life just seems as if it will be too much. You are a little overwhelmed. This is when you need to shake off the tiredness and the fear and know that you just take one bite of life at a time. To move on, you need to be brave.

Don't look at the whole picture right now. Just nibble at the edge, taking one consistent bite after another, one brave swallow after another. Most of the time, all it takes is sixty seconds of sheer bravery. If you must eat an elephant, you should start with one bite. Make one decision at a time: not to say it; to say it; to forgive right then; to pick it up; to sign up; not to eat it; to eat it; to say yes; to say no; to do it; to walk away; to run; to love to smile; to tell the truth; to apologize; to go for it; to jump; to wait. In the movie *We Bought a Zoo* the main character talks about how all one really needs in life is sixty seconds of sheer bravery and then one can do anything. That's how he meets the love of his life. When he asks her out, she says, "Why not?" Isn't that the real question, "Why not?"

Go for the gold. All you need is sixty seconds of sheer bravery one minute after the other. Don't be so exhausted by life that you are lazy. Rest well, but use that rest to give you energy and make you brave.

REFLECTION

Too much isolation and too much rest can leave you in a state of fear and sometimes laziness. If you are currently in that stage, what can you do today to shake it off and start to get back into life?

PRAYER

Lord, make me strong, brave, and confident in You. Don't let me be tired, scared, and unwilling to do anything. Lord, destroy my fear of rejection. Let me live wisely and take advantage of each moment that You give me. Give me Your energy and let me do Your will. Amen.

CONCLUSION OF SECTION VII

Rest. Rest well. Restore yourself. Give yourself grace. Give the situation grace. Rest in Jesus, and rest in the fact that He sees the big picture. He can be trusted.

Rest to get perspective. If you don't rest well, you make bad decisions.

HALT stands for hungry, angry, lonely, and tired. Halt if you are hungry, angry, lonely, or tired, and don't make rash decisions. Don't walk straight to the dump hungry, angry, lonely, and tired. If you rest well, you renew yourself—then you can skip the dump. Dumps are buggy, smelly, dirty, and nasty places. You don't want to go there.

Section VIII

DUMP

The dump is a trashy place, somewhere you don't want to be. The dump is not a nice place. Life stinks there.

Misery loves company, so if you want to be miserable, come on. If you want to be convinced not to go to the dump, then read on. In the dump you settle into your misery. Anyone who comes close to you, you tell them how awful life is. Often your breath stinks of toxic substance. You have now become a worshipper of what happened to you. You let what happened define you and take over any happy future.

On the following pages you will find devotions to help you avoid wanting to go to the dump.

Licking Your Wounds

> A person's wisdom yields patience; it is to one's glory to overlook an offense.
> —Proverbs 19:11 (NLT)

Licking your wounds is a dangerous thing to do. It just makes the wound bigger and worse. The wound stays open and never heals. Dump dwellers lick their wounds. They lick and get sick! My dog has had a spot on his paw that has been sore for about four years. He keeps licking it. He has been on antibiotics, steroids, and wound medicine countless times. He just keeps licking, licking, licking. All this licking makes the wound stay open and prevents it from healing.

It is easy to lick your wounds. I get it. Something happens or someone says something to you, and it causes a wound. It hurts. I think emotional hurts can be worse than physical hurts if you continue to dwell on them. People have doglike tendencies. The more you think about the problem, the worse it gets. You go over it in your mind and you allow it to hurt you again and again. You just keep the hurt on replay. Next, you imagine other things that people didn't actually say or didn't do, but in a warped way you convince yourself they did. Before you know it, you are in a hot mess. It hurts you much more than it should. This focus on the wound makes the wound bigger and uglier. You let it become more infected by your own memory of the hurt. The more you think about it, the more you think about it. You are letting it bring you down and not letting the wound heal. You look at your dog and watch him lick the same wound for four years. Ouch.

That is not good for anyone. The little offenses can sometimes steal more from you than the whopper offenses. With the whopper offenses, you are more aware that you need help. The little daily irritations, the snide comments, the not being included, and the self-righteous judgments of others hurt. Train your mind, heart, and soul not to take offense. Stop licking! Hurts hurt even more when you dwell on them. Hurts like these will leave you frozen in a state of misery and bitterness.

REFLECTION

Read Philippians 4:8 How can you get your mind to stop replaying past hurts?

PRAYER

Lord, let Your wisdom give me patience and kindness, and allow me to forgive others before they even hurt me. Let me forgive offenses and be forgiven when I offend others. God, make my heart so full of Your love and my status as being Your child that any power that offenses can bring will be canceled. I know I am a child of God, so petty and cruel remarks don't so easily offend me. Teach me, Lord, to let my awful wounds heal. Teach me to trust in Your promises; let me feel Your love and not allow bitterness to take hold of me. Take "replay of awful" away from me. Lord, because I am wrapped in Your love and kindness, I will rest and heal through You. I am secure in You. Do not allow me to lick my wounds or stay in a bad place. Amen.

That Is Just Plain Nasty

> Like a dog that returns to his vomit is a fool who repeats his folly.
> —Proverbs 26:11 (ESV)

You will never get out of the dump if you love your own vomit. You look at vomit and decide that you like being miserable. Being miserable and being chained by irrationality becomes your norm. It is painful to watch someone make the same mistake repeatedly. If you continue to have the same problems in each new scenario, the problem is probably you. You have a dumpy, trashy outlook.

It is heartbreaking to watch someone repeat the same follies. You want to shake them and say, *Seriously, don't do it again. No!* I have dogs, and as any good dog owner knows, they will return to their vomit and eat it. So, clean it up fast or else you are going to have to pet a dog that just ate vomit. There is a funny joke about this. One dog throws up and turns to his dog friend and says, "Hey, how cool am I? Look, I just made food," and then the dog proceeds to eat it. Returning to your vomit is nasty. It is a dense lack of understanding that causes you to repeat the same dumb mistakes again and again. Insanity is doing the same thing again and again and expecting different results. Learn from your mistakes. Better yet, be smart and learn from others' mistakes. Avoid mistakes in the first place! But if you mess up, which we all do, don't eat your vomit. Don't keep repeating the same folly! That is nasty and unintelligent!

Talking about vomit makes me want to throw up. Repeating the same mistakes is like eating vomit. Don't do it!

REFLECTION

Read 1 Corinthians 15:33-34. If you keep repeating the same mistakes, what steps can you take to stop?

PRAYER

Lord, protect me from making the same mistakes again and again. Lord, I ask You for a heart of wisdom. I ask You for a spirit of obedience to Your Word. Protect me from harm and irrationality. Get rid of the trash in my life. In Jesus's name. Amen.

Multitude of Sins

> Above all, love each other deeply, because love covers over a multitude of sins.
> —1 Peter 4:8

If you want to get out of the dump, you must forgive yourself and let go of regret. Regret likes to swirl around people's memories and brains in the dump. Regret keeps your mind on how miserable you are and how badly you have messed up or how awful your life is. Don't get high on regret; it is a very toxic substance.

Messing up is something I do a lot. The devil likes to have regrets swirl in my memory and taunt me. It's his favorite tool. God doesn't agree with this. God's favorite tools are grace and love.

Sometimes I like to play a silly game with myself because I know I have messed up so many times. If I could go back in my life to a certain time and have the chance to start over and do things differently, I would take it. I wouldn't have been so mean to boys in high school. I would have been a better wife, parent, daughter-in-law, sister-in-law, mother, daughter, sister, and friend. I would have been a better person. If only I could go back and not say some things or else say some nicer things or do things so incredibly differently that it would all be okay. But then there's this little thought in my brain that says if I could do it all again, I would just make different mistakes and have different regrets. Then I think, *Okay, I would do it again after that. I would be like the guy in the movie who just keeps reliving the same day over and over, but for me it would be the same life repeatedly.* Then I realize I will never get it right, and I pray this verse with all my heart: "Above all, love each other deeply, because love covers over a multitude of sins" (1 Peter 4:8).

Messing up is part of being human. Love is divine. When we love each other deeply, the way Christ tells us to love, this love covers over our multitude of sins. If you are holding someone captive and reminding them where they messed up, stop. Forgive. Let go. If you are making yourself a prisoner of regret, stop.

REFLECTION

Write your regrets down on a sheet of paper. Take your time. Confess, make restitution where you can, and then allow God to forgive you as you forgive yourself. Burn the paper.

PRAYER

Father, release me from regret! Forgive me and let me forgive myself and others. Let me love others deeply, and let Your love cover over my multitude of sins. Protect me, guide me, direct me. Lord, give me Your wisdom. Let Your mighty love that conquered sin and death cover my life and relationships. In Jesus's holy name. Amen.

Teachable

> For whoever has a teachable heart, to him more understanding will be given; and whoever does not have a yearning for truth, even what he has will be taken away from him.
> —Mark 4:25 (GW)

In the dump, you are not teachable. You are miserable. You are so miserable and so unreachable that people stop trying to help you because they see you don't want to be helped. You refuse help. This is an awful place to be. One of the best attributes a person can have is to be teachable. Take advice. Seek advice. Seek people who will love you so much that they will tell you the truth. Seek people who care more about you than they are concerned about hurting your feelings temporarily. Everyone should have a mentor and should serve as a mentor to someone. We all need help. We all need improvement. We all need honesty and someone to hold us accountable.

The saddest thing that can happen to a person is to become so defensive, "enlightened," educated, hurt, or offended that one can't accept advice or improve. It's as if everyone sees their zipper is down, with their junk about to show in all its glory, but no one wants to tell them for fear of getting their head bitten off. "You don't know what you don't know." Outstanding quotation! Truly, the more you see and learn, the more you realize what you don't see or don't know. The same is true of sin. The closer you get to God, the more you realize your sin and how desperately you need God. If you aren't willing to take advice, seek advice, and listen to others' well-meaning suggestions, then you are in a dangerous place.

It is very important to be teachable. Listen and seek advice. No one can know everything. People who truly love you will tell you the truth. Be teachable! Don't be so dumb that people won't bother with you anymore.

REFLECTION

Are you teachable? If not, why?

Write down what you can do right now to become more teachable. Find a Mentor, bible study, read books....

PRAYER

God, help me have a teachable heart. I ask for Your wisdom and the ability to learn. Let me seek advice and help. Discipline me when I go astray. Mold me to You. Let me give advice to others through You. Let me not easily take offense or offend others. In Jesus's holy name. Amen.

Blessings and Judgment

> Search me, God, and know my heart; test me and know my anxious thoughts. See if there is any offensive way in me and lead me in the way everlasting.
> —Psalm 139:23–24

If you really don't want to live a trashy, ugly life, you want to be judged. You want to be called out. Even though it is hard and not the way of the spirit of the world, which wants all of us not to be judged for any evil sin, it is what you need. It is a blessing. Because you have been hurt, you have allowed yourself to become a little trashy. This is where friends who truly love you are going to offer you a hand and be honest with you about all of it; take it.

"Don't judge me" is a popular saying for most of us on planet Earth, especially if we are doing something questionable. We have all been judged unfairly because of prejudice and misunderstanding, and it is painful and wicked. However, this "don't judge me" attitude we embrace can become so toxic that it allows us to harm others and tells us it is okay to be mean. If we don't stop with the bad behavior and self-permissive attitude, we will find ourselves walking around in a smelly pile of permission and meanness.

If you have ever had a good friend or been a true friend, then you know that with that friendship, you can celebrate both the blessings and judgments of life. What? Judgments? Every once in a while, we all need to be called out on our behavior. For whatever reason, we become mean, moody, vicious, bitter, and a little hateful. We justify all of this by citing what has been done to us. Then, along comes someone who truly loves us enough to tell us the truth. "Hey, you are better than that. Don't stoop to that level. Forgive, move on, and don't dwell on that anymore. What you are doing and saying is not cool. It's trashy. There is a whole beautiful world out there to enjoy, and there are many opportunities to bless others. Don't trip over this same hurtful trashy spot anymore. It's making you ugly and mean. Give it up and give it to God. Move on. Let it go."

So, you got called out. It is a good thing and you are thankful for it. Any good friend, any good parent, and God will not let you be dumb, mean, and trashy. Be thankful for both the blessings and the judgment of God and of your loyal friends. The judgments are blessings that God and your friends love you enough to help you.

REFLECTION

Do you have someone in your life who loves you enough to help you improve? If not, seek out a wiser older person to mentor you, or find an accountability partner.

PRAYER

Lord, search me and know my heart. Test me and know my anxious thoughts. Lord, see if there is an offensive way in me, and lead me in the way everlasting. Lord, convict me. Don't allow me to steep in sin and unforgiveness. Judge me, Lord. Keep me teachable and thankful for correction and advice. Bring others into my life to correct me and hold me accountable. Lord, don't let me dwell in the dump. Amen.

Written in the Sand

But Jesus went to the Mount of Olives. Early in the morning He came again to the temple. All the people came to Him, and He sat down and taught them. The scribes and the Pharisees brought a woman who had been caught in adultery, and placing her in the midst they said to Him, "Teacher, this woman has been caught in the act of adultery. Now in the Law, Moses commanded us to stone such women. So, what do You say?" This they said to test Him, that they might have some charge to bring against Him. Jesus bent down and wrote with His finger on the ground. And as they continued to ask Him, He stood up and said to them, "Let him who is without sin among you be the first to throw a stone at her." And once more He bent down and wrote on the ground. But when they heard it, they went away one by one, beginning with the older ones, and Jesus was left alone with the woman standing before Him. Jesus stood up and said to her, "Woman, where are they? Has no one condemned you?" She said, "No one, Lord." And Jesus said, "Neither do I condemn you; go, and from now on sin no more."
—John 8:1–11 (ESV)

You are surrounded by an angry mob and by evil worldly judgment everywhere you go in the dump. Because of your sin, either you are in the mob judging or you are the one being judged. This is what happens in the dump: evil, life-taking judging. This is where "judging" gets an evil reputation. This is where I agree with, "Don't judge me or others." It is easy to condemn others. It can make us look and feel better. However, it is not nice, and it is not from God. It is awful to be condemned. The good news is that people are not the judge in God's courtroom. Mercy triumphs over judgment in God's courtroom (James 2:13).

The more we live in this sinful world, the more we realize what we have done to hurt others and how much we need the forgiveness of Christ. In the story at the head of this chapter, the older ones walked away first. One of my friends in college, when we were seniors, used to say that the freshmen were so skinny compared to the seniors because the seniors had four more years of eating on them (ha-ha!). This same concept rings truer with sin: the older we are, the more years we have had to sin and mess up. That doesn't mean that sin or overeating is okay, but it does recognize the toll that living on earth can take on us. Hopefully, the more we live and experience, the more we will realize just how much we need Jesus. We don't know what Jesus wrote in the sand; it doesn't say. But if Jesus wrote the sins of the crowd in the sand for all to see, it was blown away by the wind, never to be seen again. Just like how He forgives us of our own sins. All of us at some point have probably felt like the woman caught in the act of adultery (our own shame about something), or we have found ourselves with stones in our hands, condemning others.

In my house there is a glass bowl with rocks in it. On the outside of this bowl, I have written, "Let he who is without sin throw the first rock." We need to write on our hearts and attitudes that those of us who sin (all of us) should be the first to walk away from condemning others! Let's be nice to others! Show grace, love, and forgiveness! If you are being stoned by the self-righteous religious, know that this is not from God. Repeat the verse and truth from James 2:13 over and over and out loud: Mercy triumphs over judgment!

REFLECTION

The journey of life can find us in both places described in the verse at the head of this chapter. Sometimes we can feel like the woman caught in adultery, and sometimes we can feel like one of the crowd holding the stones. Picture yourself in each of these scenarios. How can mercy triumphing over judgment change you?

PRAYER

Lord, the earth is full of sin. It separates us from You. Let us be the first to walk away from sin and the first to confess our sins. Keep us humble, honest, and aware of our desperate need for You. Thank You for cleansing us and making us whole. Thank You, God, that mercy triumphs over judgment! Don't let us run around in the dump throwing stones, being stoned, and being trashy. Amen.

The Thumb

> My plans are to prosper you and not to harm you. My plans are
> to give you hope and a future.
> —Jeremiah 29:11

So, you are finding hope again and you really want to leave the dump. You know now that God is God and you are not. Perhaps good can come out of this eventually. Laughter tickles your insides again. You are tired of the dump. There are some haughty people who think once you have visited the dump, you need to stay there. You need to stay in misery. You of all people should never laugh again. Ever! Don't listen to them. Listen to God.

A sign of healing from hard times is the ability able to joke about it. When I was with friends and joking about something that had happened to my family, they looked at me and said, "That is not funny. Don't joke about it." As if that weren't enough, one of them pulled me aside and said, "That is really not funny. We walked through that hard time with you. Don't joke about that." That is when I felt like a huge thumb from up above was coming out to squish me.

I grew up in the 1980s. I and my siblings heard so many sermons and were overly talked about in terms of what to do and what not to do. It was intense. I was so afraid of getting pregnant that I wouldn't even kiss a guy. I was petrified at the thought of messing up. Once in Sunday school, my best friend and I were supposed to act out Mary being pregnant as a teenager. The teacher said to my friend, "How would you react if your friend was pregnant? What would you say?" This was her answer: "She wouldn't be my friend if she was pregnant because my friends don't do that." Ouch. It felt as if there were this awful huge thumb hovering above my head, ready to squish me if I messed up. My mom would always say, "Nice girls don't do that or say that, and you are a nice girl, so don't do that or say that." She meant well, but again, the giant thumb was hovering.

When you are raised with well-intended strict rules, religious fear, and the desire to please everyone, it is easy to imagine that there is a thumb in the air getting ready to squish you if you mess up. Sometimes you become so concerned about pleasing others and keeping the peace that you become dysfunctional. When I fail or get chastised, I often feel like there is a big thumb squishing me hard, pushing me flat on the ground, and leaving me gasping for air. "Stay in your misery and defeat. This is where you belong!" If I listen to this voice, I get depressed. Down I'll go. I have nightmares, begin worrying, and return to my begging prayers, feeling panic that things will not be okay. I cry out to God as if He can't hear me or won't help. I feel lost and desperate.

As I was praying to God this morning, I knew He wanted to release me. This thumb picture I have in my mind is a flat-out lie from the devil. God showed me in my mind a picture of a thumb sticking up and of Him smiling. *Thumbs-up, My dear one. You don't have to stay in this mire anymore. You can laugh; it's okay. You can enjoy yourself again; it's okay. It really is okay. I want you to be happy, forgiven, whole, and blessed, to be a blessing and, most of all, to laugh. My plans are to prosper you and not to harm you. My plans are to give you hope and a future (Jeremiah 29:11). Thumbs-up, My dear one. Thumbs-up, My love. All you need is My approval, and You have it. I died for you while you were a sinner.*

REFLECTION

Take a moment to bask in the love God has for you. He is giving you a thumbs-up, and He gives you His approval. He loves you!

PRAYER

Thank You, God. I am free to leave the dump, and You, God, are holding my hand and leading the way. Your mercy triumphs over judgment. Amen.

Taking Out the Trash

> For if you forgive other people when they sin against you, your heavenly Father will also forgive you. But if you do not forgive others their sins, your Father will not forgive your sins.
> —Matthew 6:14–15

After you have outgrown clothing or have used a milk carton, you don't hold onto that clothing or empty milk carton as if it owes you something. If you are smart, you let it go. You pass the clothing to the next person, and you put the milk carton into the recycling bin. You let it become the next thing it is meant to be. If you were to hold onto that piece of clothing or milk carton and carry it around everywhere, that would be weird.

On a personal level, consider that your personal story is sad. You have had a lot of bad things happen. Life has beaten you down. It has been unfair. You have been lied to, manipulated, and used, or have just made decisions that have made life feel like a dump. You can carry this burden with you if you want. It's a very heavy load to carry everywhere you go. Forgiving is hard. It is a two-way street where you keep bumping into yourself. You need to either forgive or be forgiven. If you don't forgive, you just keep tripping over your trash. I wish that I could just forgive once and be done, then everything would be all good. I wouldn't ever think about the offense, never dwell on it, and just go on my merry way as happy as a lark.

Unfortunately, that is not how things play out for me. For me, forgiving has been more like taking out my trash. If I take it out every day, I do much better. If I let it pile up, both I and the trash begin to smell bad. Forgiveness for me has been a daily event, and sometimes a moment-by-moment event. I have to repeat:

"God forgave me and told me to forgive others. Not because they deserve it, but because it sets me free. I don't deserve forgiveness. I forgive you because God forgave me."

Forgiving is a messy business. I think I'm all done with a particular situation, but then I still bump into that terrible memory and that hard place at the bottom of my heart. I must pick up that trash and take it out again.

Eventually it will all be gone. Until then, I will just keep forgiving and picking up any trash I find. I repeat, "God forgives me; therefore, I forgive you."

REFLECTION

Are you good at taking out your trash daily? Write out how you can start to get rid of your trash.

PRAYER

Lord, forgive me for holding on to forgiveness like a power trip. When unforgiveness tries to sneak back in, let me repeat and remember: I don't deserve forgiveness. You died for me while I was a sinner. You set me free to be in fellowship with You. I release forgiveness to others. Lord, let me forgive right away, all the way, and with a grateful heart. Make forgiveness a way of life for me so an unforgiving spirit won't have me in bondage. Thank You, Lord. Amen!

Letting Go

> When I was a child, I talked like a child, I thought like a child,
> I reasoned like a child. When I became a man, I put the ways
> of childhood behind me.
> —1 Corinthians 13:11

If you are a parent, when your kids are in the dump, you feel as if you are too. When you go to this dumpy place, you aren't helping anyone. Now all of you are in a bad place. The quote "You're only as happy as your happiest kid," which I think is false, has been a very hard lie for me to get over. I swallowed the lie whole. When my kids hurt, I hurt, sometimes more than they do

A mother eagle makes the best nest for her sweet eaglets. It is warm, cozy, and safe on top. She sits on the eggs, then when they hatch, provides everything the little eaglets need nonstop. She keeps them warm and safe and destroys any potential enemies. It is her job. As they get older, she pulls out some soft feathers and cozy layers. Rocks show, and then it is not so comfortable for those little eaglets. The eaglets keep growing and become ready to begin thinking about their future. The wise eagle continues to pull out the soft material from her nest, which exposes glass and other sharp objects. These little eaglets are ready to fly, and it is time to let them do so. She is wise and by instinct builds the nest like this on purpose. If things are too comfortable and every need is met, those eaglets will never grow up and become great eagles. She needs to let them go. She needs to force them out. Sometimes she even gives them a push out of the nest because she knows they can fly on their own.

Deep down we know our kids can fly on their own, too. We also must release them or nuzzle them out of the nest. We need to be strong, trust God, and not let their happiness be our happiness. Otherwise it is not healthy. Yes, pray for them, encourage them, and be there for them, but let go. Make your own happiness because that teaches them to grow up and to respect you, your time, and your resources. It allows you to become adult friends. It's perfectly normal for your kids to visit the dump. Just don't go there with them. Let them fly, fall, mess up, and learn all on their own.

REFLECTION

How can you avoid being in the dump when those you love are in the dump?

What do you need to let go of?

PRAYER

Lord, in 1 Corinthians 13:11 it says: "When I was a child, I talked like a child; I thought like a child, I reasoned like a child. When I became a man, I put the ways of childhood behind me." Lord, I give You my children. They are adults. Let them be mighty, strong, healthy, and God-fearing adults who love You and do Your will. Get rid of any unhealthy childhood dependency on me. Let me respect them as adults, and let them respect me as an older adult. Don't let me go to the dump with them. Amen.

Shots of Poison

> In Him we have redemption through His blood, the forgiveness of sins, in accordance with the riches of God's grace.
> —Ephesians 1:7

So, are you going to keep sitting at the bar in the dump where the devil serves the drinks? I have a friend who infuriates me because she won't forgive herself. She messed up badly in a situation and can't forgive herself for it. It is as if by condemning herself even more and constantly feeling bad about herself, she can make it right again. She gives grace to everyone else, but not to herself. She knows Jesus but for some reason won't allow Him to forgive her. She has shackled herself to some serious pain.

Drinking shots of poison is how I describe someone who can't forgive. They either can't forgive themselves or can't forgive others. Every hour or so, they take another shot of condemnation, judgment, and punishment. They think that by drinking this, they are getting what they deserve, namely, misery, or what others deserve—also misery. The only people they are really making miserable and sick are themselves and anyone who gets too close. It is very arrogant and self-absorbed. Everyone else can forgive and be forgiven, but they can't. They are too proud to be forgiven or to forgive. It must give them some kind of sick control. They just continue to sit at the bar in the dump where the devil is the bartender and his favorite shot to serve is syrupy, sticky, poisonous unforgiveness.

Stop poisoning yourself with unforgiveness. It's making you sick. Jesus died on the cross for our sins. Don't let His redemption of you go to waste. Forgive.

REFLECTION

Do you need to stop drinking poison? What is in the poison that you are drinking?

To leave the dump, you need to forgive. What do you need to forgive yourself or others for?

PRAYER

Lord, unshackle me from unforgiveness. I receive Your mercy, grace, and forgiveness. Allow me to give Your mercy, grace, and forgiveness to others. You came to give us life and life abundantly. I accept. I am forgiven. I forgive. Amen.

Treats

> Taste and see that the Lord is good; blessed is the one who takes refuge in Him.
> —Psalm 34:8

If I could help get you out of the dump, I would leave a trail of shiny treats for you that would lead you to the forgiveness door. Sometimes in life we have had so many sour experiences that we forget that the Lord is good. Sadly, we watch those we love who have been extremely hurt forget that they are loved by God. They don't even believe in God anymore.

I went on a five thirty sunrise walk where God displayed His full glory in a pink sunrise splashing with waves, and I felt full of joy. It was hard not to be in awe of God's handiwork. My sister, Kerry, was teaching her new puppy, Annie, how to behave. She brought a bag full of cut-up hot dogs. Kerry had her sweet little puppy eat little bites and stay right with her. After walking awhile, the puppy would get curious about a seagull or a person coming our way. Kerry would call Annie to come, and that cute puppy would come so fast that she would leave skid marks in the sand. Annie knew she was loved and safe and that she would get a treat. Being next to Kerry was a good thing, and Annie knew it. No temptation was worth not being next to her owner.

During this walk, I felt my heart ache for someone I was praying for whose heart was broken. We all need to taste and see that the Lord is good. We need to be so close to God and realize how great He is that nothing else distracts us. Just like Annie the dog knew her owner was good, we know God is so good that nothing is worth being separated from Him: not the skimpily clad people on the beach; not the trashy things in life that look very tempting; not the rotting dead fish that smells so good (anything toxic to humans) to us, offers lies, and causes us to smell bad; and not other people we think we need to get our happiness from. No hurt or pain, no sadness, and no sickness or disease can separate us from God!

A bitter soul is not good. God is good, and sometimes we need to see His goodness! God, show us Your goodness.

REFLECTION

What does the "goodness of God" mean to you?

How can you share the goodness of God in such a way that people can receive it?

PRAYER

O Lord, give _____ [name of person you are praying for or yourself] such treats, love, and fellowship with You that _____ wants to be in Your presence. Remove the lies and temptations that offer temporary relief. God, let _____ know You are good. Let _____ taste and see that You are good. Lord, let _____'s heart overflow with Your love. Bless _____ . Bring _____ close to You. Let _____ know Your love, grace, and glory. Lord, let _____ take refuge in You. Be _____'s safe place. May _____ know that You are good! In Jesus's holy name. Amen.

CONCLUSION OF SECTION VIII

Dumps are trashy places. If you are in a dump, then leave!
Leave the dump through the door of forgiveness.

Section IX

FORGIVENESS

Forgive, O my love, forgive. It sets you free.
If we don't forgive, either someone else or ourselves, we will sit with other bitter souls in a dark, dank corner and be unable to see the light.

After experiencing betrayal, we may endure the hardest, darkest of times. Those folks were supposed to be like Jesus—they had religious robes on them—and what we experienced was some evil and falsehood.

Don't ever forget who the true enemy really is: the devil!

When you stop blaming people and situations, that is when you heal, even if the hurt is still going on. You stop and realize it was never really the people or the situation; it was the devil doing his work through people and the situation.

You can forgive people because, like you, they are human.

The real enemy has always been the devil and always will be.

On the following pages you will find devotions to help you forgive and be forgiven.

Sitting in the Dank Corner

> Then you will be handed over to be persecuted and put to death, and you will be hated by all nations because of Me. At that time many will turn away from the faith and will betray and hate each other, and many false prophets will appear and deceive many people. Because of the increase of wickedness, the love of most will grow cold, but the one who stands firm to the end will be saved. And this gospel of the kingdom will be preached in the whole world as a testimony to all nations, and then the end will come.
> —Matthew 24:9–14

If you don't forgive, you will sit in a dank corner of misery. One of my friends has been miserable for a long time. For years, she has been sick, having had some disappointments, feeling betrayed, and being unhappy. Because of all this, she doesn't believe in God anymore. She sits in a dank corner, hurting and untrusting. I wish I could get her to stand up and see the loving eyes of Jesus.

People who have been hurt and betrayed by religion and fake people are some of the hardest people to reach. They trusted and hoped in a system where people lied to them, ate them up, and spit them out. Even when God shows up, they feel so bamboozled, hoodwinked, fooled, abused, misrepresented, unforgiven, bitter, angry, and mad that they can't see past their pain. God is right there, but they are so huddled in their hurt and pain that they can't see Him.

Because of pain of this nature, we wrap ourselves up in hurt, education, and experience and choose what we want to believe and hear. Even when someone is kind, we mistakenly believe it to be fake or judgmental. Worse yet, we make ourselves feel as if we don't deserve kindness or favor. We sit in a dirty, smelly barn, complaining about all our hurts and the people who have sinned against us, saying that this God thing cannot be true. We sit on the edge of paradise complaining. It's an awful feeling to feel like that. Let this be a warning to your soul: don't get bitter; forgive quickly; get over it; brush yourself off; and don't be so educated and enlightened that you are dumb!

Know that there are false prophets and fake, mean Christians. Don't let the pain they caused you to separate you from the one true God. Be smart.

Now, brush yourself off and get out of the dank corner, for crying out loud! Stand up and see the eyes of your loving Father God. He is waiting to embrace you and welcome you into His peace and paradise!

"You will receive a rich welcome into the eternal kingdom of our Lord and Savior Jesus Christ" (2 Peter 1:11).

REFLECTION

Unforgiveness can wrap its ugly tentacles all over you and keep you bound in bitterness. It robs you of life. If you have unforgiveness in your life, do you realize that this is what is keeping you bound? Do you want to give your hurts and pain that much power?

PRAYER

Lord, I look forward to seeing You. God, keep me from false ways and from embracing the ways and lies of the world. I ask for your divine protection from evil. Make me wise. Let me take refuge in You. Keep me faithful. Hug me tight. Amen.

Notice: Scapegoat Season Closed Permanently

> So, if the Son sets you free, you are free indeed.
> —John 8:36

Finding someone to blame, blaming yourself, or being blamed is wrong. Forgiveness happened on the cross. Forgiveness is always in season. None of us wants to be guilty, and we don't want to be blamed. It's so much easier to blame someone else. Scapegoating is so much easier. Don't do it, and don't accept it.

You can find the original scapegoat in the Bible on the Day of Atonement. A goat was sent into the wilderness after the Jewish chief priest had symbolically laid the sins of the people on this goat (see Leviticus 16). If you think that is cruel, read about the other goat. Two goats were picked to atone for sins. One was sacrificed for the people's sins, and the other had the sins of the people placed on it and was let loose in the wilderness. If you were a goat in those days, it was a rough life, and you did not want to be picked on the Day of Atonement. You were innocent, yet you took on all the Israelites' sins. You died immediately, or possibly starved, or got eaten in the wilderness with everyone's sins placed upon you.

Because God wants fellowship with each human through Jesus Christ's love and death on the cross, we are all offered the ultimate scapegoat in Jesus, who died on the cross for all our sins. No more animal sacrifices ever! No more scapegoats ever! Jesus said with His dying breath on the cross, "It is finished" (John 19:30). With His ultimate authority, scapegoat season was closed forever. If you have been a scapegoat for someone else or you are punishing yourself for your own sins, you are being told lies directly from the devil. Jesus died on the cross for your sins. All you must do is ask Jesus to come into your heart and take your sins away. It is that simple. No more condemnation. If you are scapegoating someone by putting your sins, misplaced anger, and blame on that person, stop. You are wasting your energy, time, and relationships. If you are punishing yourself for your own sins, stop! All you need to do is look in the mirror, confess, and give your sins to Jesus.

He forgives you. He forgave you before you committed the sins. You can only control yourself. Forgive yourself and let God do the rest.

We waste so much energy trying to find someone to blame, punish, and ultimately ostracize. This is so incredibly shameful. If you are in a church or in a relationship that scapegoats and ostracizes others, you should know that these folks do not know the real Jesus. Leave. Most churches and people who say they love Jesus should have a sign posted: Notice: Scapegoat Season Is Closed Forever!

Look in the mirror and confess your sins. Accept Jesus's forgiveness. Own up. Pray for your enemies. Forgive those who hurt you. No blaming here. Own up and say, "I am forgiven, and I forgive!" Say it out loud. Be released. You can control only yourself. Jesus is the ultimate scapegoat forever and ever. Love one another as Jesus has loved you. Do not be a scapegoat or become someone else's scapegoat!

REFLECTION

Do you always need someone to blame when problems arise?

What can you do to take responsibility for yourself and own your situations, then move on and make better choices in the future?

PRAYER

Lord, thank You for the promise in John 8:36 that if the Son sets one free, one is free indeed. Lord, my shame is nailed on Your cross. Thank You. Jesus, You set me free! I will run, frolic, and rejoice in Your love, mercy, and freedom. Amen.

Stones versus Flesh

> I will give you a new heart and put a new spirit in you; I will remove from you your heart of stone and give you a heart of flesh.
> —Ezekiel 36:26

A raging battle is going on inside your heart, one that you think will be won with a stone like David's when he took down Goliath, but you find this battle is only won when you let go of the stone. Let this stone drop to the ground like the ones held by the crowd who decided not to stone the woman caught in adultery. They dropped their stones and walked away. Those who were without sin were supposed to throw the first stone. No one could do it. No one was innocent. No one was without sin. Mercy triumphs over judgment. Come on, drop the stone. Let it go. Let forgiveness talk to you.

At some point in our lives, we tire of being lonely and miserable. We look at ourselves and wonder if our young selves were to bump into our current selves, would we be shocked and disappointed? We miss what it felt like when we had a heart of flesh rather than a stony heart. We have all felt it before, the hardening of our hearts. It is a feeling we feel deep within our souls. It arises because of rejection, death, a mean word, unemployment, or being too short, too tall, too fat, or too small. The list goes on. We scream in our hearts, *I've had enough!* and cry out, "You will never, ever hurt me like this again!"

Sometimes, counselors advise us to shut the door and cut people off. It feels empowering to protect ourselves like this. The problem is that the problem often doesn't stop at that one relationship or situation. We become defensive and careful not to let anyone hurt us like that again. We don't take risks anymore. Often our hearts and potential future relationships are blockaded by this hard-hearted attitude. We don't hear people say hi to us, we keep our heads down, tears often spring from our souls and we are lonely. Deep, sad impenetrable anger and loneliness follows us like a cloud. Others can't reach us. Ever so slowly we find we have stone-cold hearts. Something needs to change in our hearts, or else our very beings might crumble from the heaviness. We need an encounter with ourselves face-to-face in the mirror.

You don't like what you see? How did you get like this? "I am God, and you are not," resounds deep within your soul. Your usual intellectual answers to this are now strangely silent. Slowly, forgiveness leans in. You sit down and have a long heart-to-heart talk with forgiveness. Forgiveness is the only thing that can save you. Tears spring from your soul. You feel love. You feel overwhelmingly loved. You find forgiveness for those who hurt you; you forgive yourself; and you forgive God. You feel this deep within you. There is a realization that who you are and the idea of who you want to be needs to change. You ask God for an operation that removes the stone in your heart and replaces it with flesh. Understanding forgiveness that isn't deserved is a new thing to you. You repeat the command from Colossians 3:13 over and over in your heart: "God forgave me, so I can forgive them." This becomes your mantra. You don't become dumb. You just become wise. You pray for a hedge of protection, but not for a hard heart. You feel unshackled, free at last. Empowered by love.

God can remove your heart of stone and give you a heart of flesh. Let Him operate. Close your eyes and ask God to take away your heart of stone and give you a heart of flesh. Ask Him to operate. Let Ezekiel 36:26 speak to you: "I will give you a new heart and put a new spirit in you; I will remove from you your heart of stone and give you a heart of flesh."

REFLECTION

In Proverbs 4:23, it says: "Above all else, guard your heart, for everything you do flows from it." The hardening of your heart can happen so subtly that you don't even realize it is occurring. If you need a heart operation from God, let Him operate! Write out what you think God needs to remove. Next, let Him do His work.

After the operation, what can you do to prevent your heart from getting hard again?

PRAYER

God, I am asking You to give me an operation and change my heart of stone to a heart of flesh. Change me, Lord. Take away all bitterness, hate, regret, and unforgiveness, and any worship of terrible memories. Scrape out the ick that is attached to me. Forgive me, Lord. Let me forgive. Operate. Help me feel love, help me forgive, and help me trust You. Wrap me in Your Holy Spirit and heal me. Thank You. Amen.

Forgive Me!

> Yours, O Lord, is the greatness, the power, the glory, the victory, and the majesty. Everything in the heavens and on earth is Yours, O Lord, and this is Your kingdom. We adore You as the one who is over all things. Wealth and honor come from You alone, for You rule over everything. Power and might are in Your hand, and at Your discretion people are made great and given strength.
> —1 Chronicles 29:11–13 (ESV)

I need forgiveness. I have failed to live as if God owns all of heaven and earth, and because of that I really hurt my friend. Oh, it's hard to be in human skin. Humans are selfish and self-centered. We desperately need God to protect us from being so selfish!

I must share one of my worst moments when I was incredibly slow-witted, embarrassing, and shallow. I was leading a Bible study at my home. The Bible study had been together for about three years. My husband had been without a job for almost two years. We had both worked odd jobs, done some consulting, and gone without. I had an almost three-year-old and quite frankly was worn out. We were out of money. "Self-absorbed in my woes" perfectly describes my state of mind! Not that any of this makes what I did okay. It wasn't okay. At the end of Bible study, we were sharing prayer requests, and one woman asked us to pray that her husband would get an outstanding job. He had just graduated from law school. I don't even want to tell you what I said. It is very embarrassing and mean. I didn't even remember saying it until she told me about it. I said, "We can't pray for him to have a job until my husband has a job."

Did I really say that? How incredibly shallow and selfish! I think I must have thought God had a limited supply of jobs that could be handed out or prayers that He could answer. Shame on me! Did I not know everything in heaven and earth belongs to God? I didn't even remember saying this. It took my friend's not showing up at dinner club and Bible study for a month for me to realize how much I had hurt her. Finally, I asked her if something was wrong. She burst into tears and told me what I had said. Shame and embarrassment filled my being! "I am so sorry. Shame on me!" were the only words I could say. I had been very self-absorbed, not realizing how big God is and not trusting in a God who can count all the hairs on our heads and take care of all of us. Ugh to me! He has an unlimited supply; He owns it all.

I am telling you this story to bring my cavalier self down a couple of notches. How in the world could I have been so absolutely dumb and self-absorbed? Then, I think of all the times I haven't voiced my selfish thoughts:

- *It's my turn, God.*
- *I have been praying for a baby. Why does she get to have all those kids and You won't give me any?*
- *Don't You care, God? Why does everything go so right for them, and You won't help me?*

O so many selfish thoughts that want to convince me that God has a limited supply of jobs, gifts, blessings, and love. He owns it all. He is all. He has enough for everyone. It's hard to be in human skin.

REFLECTION

God owns all of heaven and earth. He is enough. He has enough. When you can celebrate that others have the things you wish you had, that is true trust and belief in a God that loves you.

How can you celebrate and pray for others even if God doesn't answer your prayers in that same area?

PRAYER

Holy Father, forgive me for my selfishness and for my lack of understanding of how great You are. Let me truly understand that everything in heaven and earth belongs to You. I am just passing through. You have enough. You are enough. Let me rest in You. Father, please don't let me offend or hurt others. God, keep me from evil so I will not harm others or myself. Please give me a hedge of protection so I won't hurt others and be self-centered. Heal any whom I have hurt. Let Your mighty grace and mercy prevail. Take all lies of the enemy away from me. You are in charge. You are God and I am not. In Jesus's holy name. Amen.

My Bad

> Therefore, confess your sins to each other and pray for each other so that you may be healed. The prayer of a righteous person is powerful and effective.
> —James 5:16

Humility and forgiveness often hold hands and surround those who have humble, forgiving hearts. This makes life worth living. This is the good stuff. Being humble and saying one is sorry are two of the best things a person can do.

One of the many things I like about my dad is his humility and his ability to say he is sorry. After many weary days of traveling for work, he came into my room when I was about seven and asked how I was doing. I told him my gerbil died. He said, "That's nice, dear." A few days later he came in and asked me where my gerbil was. I said, "I told you he died, and you said, 'That's nice, dear.'" He got on his knees and said, "I am so sorry. I must have been tired and wasn't listening." He gave me a big, long hug and kept saying he was sorry. That is one of many memories I have of him apologizing.

One of my kids' friends heard me apologizing to my son. No offense, but his mom rails on him. He is a handful; I'll give her that. But she is always talking about what a troublemaker he is. I am not sure her talking about it so much helps the situation. It makes me sad. This young man said to me, "I would do anything to hear my mom say she is sorry." Teaching our kids we are not perfect is a priceless gift. By setting the example by teaching our kids to say they're sorry and admit when they are wrong, we are giving them a pertinent life skill.

Being humble is one of the most attractive qualities a person can have. Thank you, Dad.

REFLECTION

Is it really that hard to forgive and say you are sorry? What keeps you from walking in humility?

PRAYER

God, help me be humble. Let me apologize, see others' points of view, and most of all love like You do. Lord, love others through me. Amen.

Forgive First

> The discretion of a man defers his anger; and it is his glory to pass over a transgression.
> —Proverbs 19:11 (NKJV)

If you are quick to forgive, you are mature and living life like a hero! Be the first to say you are sorry. Always! You are the bigger person if you apologize first!

When my kids were little, I would tell them often always to be the first to apologize. The one who is first to apologize is the more mature person. Sometimes I would give my children a little award if they would say they were sorry first. Many times when an apology is needed in a situation, there is a standoff. Both parties are guilty and need to say they are sorry. It is like they circle each other and growl, waiting on the other one to break down and admit they were wrong. In reality, you both are wrong, and you both know it. You know what? The bigger, more emotionally mature person always says he or she is sorry first. This person knows the relationship is more important than determining who is right and who is wrong.

Always be the one to forgive first.

REFLECTION

The next time you forgive first, give yourself an award! Treat yourself! Good job!

PRAYER

Lord, demolish my pride, arrogance, and desire to be right. Let me always care more about the person in front of me than being right. Help me be the first to apologize. Amen.

Grace Bombs

> For it is by grace you have been saved, through faith—and this is not from yourselves, it is the gift of God—not by works, so that no one can boast.
> —Ephesians 2:8–9

The world needs grace bombs, a gigantic explosion of forgiveness! Grace is undeserved mercy. A grace bomb is an explosion of mercy, love, and forgiveness.

I have three boys, now men. Grace bombs were an extremely important part of their upbringing. We would slowly act out a make-believe bomb exploding in our hands and say, "Grace bomb!" In my mind it was like love, mercy, and forgiveness had just exploded all over the place. Boys like bombs, and I like bombs that are full of grace, love, mercy, and forgiveness. This tradition started because every once in a while, I wanted my kids to experience complete forgiveness when they really should have been in trouble. "Grace bomb!" I didn't do it all the time, but they loved it when I did.

Grace is what God gives us. We should be in a time-out and, even worse, Hades, but we aren't because God came and died for us while we were sinners. Did you hear that? He died for us while we were doing something bad! Who does that? Only God. I am not God, but I wanted my children to know how much He truly loves them, just to experience a complete overwhelming gigantic *grace bomb*: a grace bomb explosion full of undeserving, unexpected, blown-away-by grace. Now that they are older, *grace bomb* has taken on a complete new teenage tone. You know when you get to a point where you just can't see eye to eye? You have both said things you shouldn't and neither one can totally give in to the other's side? It's a standoff. That is when one of my kids or me will say we need a grace bomb. We will just let it go, forgive each other, even though we each think we are so completely right and the other person is totally misguided and wrong. Grace bomb! Let the relationship and fellowship be restored. Heal. Agree to disagree. Grace. It is really all about the relationship after all.

Let a grace bomb go off in your relationships. It is so much fun and is healing!

REFLECTION

God gave us the ultimate grace bomb by having Jesus die for our sins. Throw out some grace bombs today to others (especially if they don't deserve it).

If you were to use a grace bomb when it is needed, how would that change you and others?

PRAYER

Lord, thank You for undeserved grace. Thank You that while we are sinners, Christ died for us. Thank You for the fact that we can't earn grace. Lord, I ask that a complete grace bomb go off in my attitude and in Your world. God, let forgiveness and kindness reign. Let me reflect Your love and grace to others. Amen.

CONCLUSION OF SECTION IX

You and forgiveness have become such good friends that you now hold the door for each other before you enter new situations. Sometimes, forgiveness enters first and prepares you to forgive others before they even hurt you. Sometimes forgiveness helps you laugh things off.

Forgiveness likes to dance. Forgiveness has been dancing in the surrounding air up and down throughout your journey, even when you were in the pit of despair. Forgiveness has asked you to dance repeatedly. Since you finally accepted the dance with forgiveness, you are happy and full of a peace that passes understanding. You and forgiveness dance all the time together. You really enjoy each other's company, and laughter is your primary form of communication.

Forgiveness is so kind, it invites you to attend a picnic with Never Mind.

Section X

NEVER MIND

Just sit with me, my love.
Let's delight in each other's company at the picnic of "never mind."

Forgiveness explains that very few people get to partake in this delicious picnic, and you feel blessed for the invitation. "Never mind" is the best place to be. You have finally gotten to the place in life where Jesus is your best friend, and it really does not matter what others think. Your goal is to bring glory to God. Your friendship with God is of the utmost importance, and you really don't care about pleasing humans; it is all about pleasing the Lord. You are at a wonderful "never mind" place.

On the following pages you will find devotions about the "never mind" disposition; the Lord is first in your life.

I. Don't. Care

Teach us to number our days, that we may gain a heart of wisdom.
—Psalm 90:12

On the "never mind" mountain, you finally realize it's wonderful to be you. You do what God created you to do. You don't have to focus on things that rob you of life. In fact, you don't. You're smart.

The older I get, the more I realize I don't have to take part in things that are life-robbing and mundane, pious muck. Therefore, sometimes I just don't care, nor do I want to. I'm not being rude; I'm being honest and releasing myself from bondage obligations!

"I. Don't. Care!" This is one of my favorite lines from a movie ever, *Remember the Titans*. One coach's little girl is a huge football fan. She could coach the team and does so from the sidelines. The other coach's daughter has brought her dolls to the game and isn't the least bit interested in the game. They are both in the football stands, and the girl who loves football is going ballistic on the sidelines. She is coaching and screaming and turns to the other little girl to rant about an unfair call by the referee. The little girl looks at her as she combs her doll's hair and states, "I. Don't. Care. Did you hear me? I. Don't. Care!" That line is so funny. My sister and I repeat it all the time. I text it to her and her to me, especially if we are in or around a life-draining situation. (Use your imagination: mandatory meetings, someone who talks way too much, people who actually waste our time talking about how many ice cubes would look nice in the lemonade). Seriously, there are only twenty-four hours in a day and sixty seconds in a minute, and there are some things I really don't care about.

Here is the deal: we only have so much time in a day, and I consider all my time valuable. In life we need to choose our "I care"s and "I don't care"s carefully. They won't all be the same for all of us. We are all made with a unique design and with unique aptitudes.

Use your time wisely. Don't get robbed by things that are mundane, pious, boring, and draining. It is okay not to go, not to play politics, to say no, and to tell people politely that such-and-such is an area that does not suit you.

If it is not beneficial to God, you, or someone else, then why waste your time? The only thing that is mandatory is birth and death. Other than that, God gives you the choice and the aptitude.

REFLECTION

Do you have bondage obligations? List them. God made us all different. Give yourself freedom not to do things.

PRAYER

Lord, teach us to number our days that we may get hearts of wisdom. Let us not waste our time and resources. Let us be confident in what You gave us to do and in our unique God-given abilities. Lord, protect us from squandering our lives away on things that really don't matter and trying to please others. Let my yes be a yes and my no be a no. Make my will be Your will, and Your will be my will. Amen.

Rejoice!

> Rejoice in the Lord always. Again, I say, rejoice! Let everyone see your gentleness. The Lord is near! Do not be anxious about anything. Instead, in every situation, through prayer and petition with thanksgiving, tell your requests to God. And the peace of God that surpasses all understanding will guard your hearts and minds in Christ Jesus.
> —Philippians 4:4–7 (ESV)

Times of celebrating and praising the Lord become your happiest moments on the "never mind" mountain. Life may not be perfect, but God is good and worthy of praise. When my children are grateful and appreciative, it makes me want to do more for them. Then I think about how much God wants to hear "Thank You" from us.

One of the most fun parts about being a parent is when your kid's being thankful turns into true rejoicing. It is a delightful blessing to witness. The verse Philippians 4:7 is so fun! The fact that it repeats twice that we need to rejoice is freeing and feels like an invitation to celebrate! Sometimes things are so great that we need to say them twice. Rejoice! Rejoice! Woo-hoo!

Recently, I bought myself a tambourine. It makes me happy. When no one is home, I like to get that tambourine and do a little dance. I turn up the music loud and have a big time. It is fun and freeing and puts me in a wonderful state of mind. I think about all I am thankful for, and my body just wants to praise dance. When David was celebrating the ark being brought back (1 Chronicles 15:26–29), he really did a jig—complete praise, unabandoned joy, and total worship. The word *rejoice* means to feel great joy or delight. What fun. Rejoice, celebrate, and think of everything you have to be thankful for. Take out a tambourine and dance for the Lord with a grateful, joy-filled heart.

The tambourine is the easiest instrument to play. You just shake it and tap it. Just like a tambourine is easy to use, rejoicing is easy too. Put on some great praise dancing music, think about all you are thankful for, and dance, praise, celebrate, and rejoice! Rejoice! Spread around contagious joy in your life! Dance for the Lord with a grateful, joyful heart!

REFLECTION

Today, put on some praise music and dance with the Lord.

PRAYER

God, holy, holy are You, Lord, who was, and is, and is to come. Everything in heaven and earth belongs to You. You are mighty and worthy of praise. Nothing is impossible for You. You love me very much. Your precious Son died on the cross to give me a life with You. You protect me. You are good. I celebrate Your tender mercy and grace. Thank You for Your forgiveness of my sins. Thank You for counting the hairs on my head. Thank You that nothing can separate me from Your love. Thank You for the fact that every knee will bow to you and every heart will confess that You are the only true God. Thank You for the gift of life. Thank You for loving me. My heart bubbles over with praise. I will dance with joy and gladness in Your presence. I love You, God. May I dance every day with the joy of the Lord and with thankfulness in my heart to You, God! Amen.

Joke Night, because Even if Things Are Not Okay, It's Okay to Laugh—It's Healing!

> A merry heart does good, like medicine, but a broken spirit dries the bones.
> —Proverbs 17:22 (KJV)

When you enter the state of "never mind," you realize how important laughter is. You pursue joy. For many years, Monday night was joke night in our family. The first person to make me laugh got five dollars or a back rub—their choice. Monday is usually the hardest day to get through for most people. You just finished a cozy, restful weekend, and you're back into the thick of things. A rainy Monday is even harder; it is like a wet fish slap across your face, changing your entire demeanor. So, sometimes you need to be intentional and deliberately bring laughter into your life.

Joke night started when one of my kids was severely sick. His thyroid numbers were out of normal range by a dangerously high two hundred points. He was told by the doctor to come home from college. His coloring was gray. It is a long, slow process to get your thyroid and TSH levels right. If you increase the medicine too fast, you will die of a heart attack. Sometimes it takes years to get your levels right. I was reading every book, article, and website I could find to locate answers and get help. It was heart wrenching. Laughter kept coming up as a healing agent. Laughter literally releases good hormones into your body. So in our family, we told jokes and watched funny movies and videos; we tried to keep it light; and we prayed for healing.

When your spirit breaks, it dries your bones. That's a scary visual, especially for me as I get older. I try to laugh, tell jokes, and watch funny shows. Everyone should know a good, clean funny joke and be able to tell it at the spur of the moment. Being able to laugh, enjoy life, and lighten the atmosphere is healing. Laughter is healing. It is like an expensive delightful perfume for your soul and your well-being.

REFLECTION

Write down ways you can bring laughter into your heart and relationships. Make it a goal to pursue joy.

PRAYER

Lord, give me a pleasant sense of humor. Let me not take life so seriously. Let me be able to laugh. Let me laugh at myself and delight in Your world. Let me have a merry heart. In Jesus's name.

Who

> Now faith is confidence in what we hope for and assurance about what we do not see.
> —Hebrews 11:1

When you understand who you are and whose you are, you don't have to worry so much about what happens. You are on the wonderful "never mind" mountain. Here, you trust God. God is more concerned about who you are than about what you have to go through. He can see your entire life (past, present, and future) and knows what's best.

Have you ever prayed for God to give you a clear path? I have. You just want things to go smoothly. Ease would be so nice after many turnarounds, uphills, and scraped knees. I recently went on a hike when the weather was extremely foggy. I could see about three feet ahead and that was it. Thick fog surrounded me. I did that same hike a year ago, and it started out foggy and then cleared up and was beautiful. Last year, it was as if God was showing me to walk by faith, not by sight, and then I got the privilege of seeing the mountain views and flowers as I felt His peace. This year, on this familiar annual hike, it stayed foggy. The wisdom of God swirled in my thoughts: "Sometimes the fog is here for your protection. I've got you. If you could see the path I am taking you on, you might not go. You would be overcome with fear and the desire to stay safe. Right now, all you need is to see right in front of you. I'll show you the views in good time. The path I am taking you on is for your own good. This path is going to be part of your story. This path is going to determine who you become."

God is more interested in the who than in the how. That's a true blessing. We don't have to understand the why and most often won't. It's okay; the who is more important. The who is a person who is humble, kind, and thoughtful, an overcomer who empathizes, works hard, and is thankful, appreciative, generous, trusting, and forgiving and who takes time for others and trusts God. I'll take that kind of who any day over someone whose life has gone perfect yet who can't relate to us "who"s who struggle and overcome. (Yes, I am referring to Dr. Seuss's Whos.)

Our family and extended family have a call to find each other in the woods or crowded places. We sound like owls. "Who, who, who, who" (we sing this to the tune of "Who cooks for you?"). We answer back "Who, who" (to the tune of "You do"). From now on when I use this call, I am going to remember in my soul that no matter what we have all gone through or will go through, God, who is good and worthy of praise, cares more about the who than about the how.

REFLECTION

Are you able to praise God because He is more concerned about the who than about the how, even if the how is hard? Why or why not?

PRAYER

Lord, faith is the confidence in what we hope for and assurance about what we do not see. Just as a Bible verse can teach us so many facets of You, we are not limited in our faith to a formula or the same answer or experience as last time. You are good. Thank You for caring more about the who than about the how. Let us trust that You make us into the best "who"s ever! Amen.

Pilate's Final Say

> Pilate had a notice prepared and fastened to the cross. It read: "Jesus of Nazareth, the King of the Jews." Many of the Jews read this sign, for the place where Jesus was crucified was near the city, and the sign was written in Aramaic, Latin, and Greek. The chief priests of the Jews protested to Pilate, "Do not write 'The King of the Jews,' but that this man claimed to be king of the Jews." Pilate answered, "What I have written, I have written."
> —John 19:19–22

In our politically charged atmosphere, no matter who is in charge, God oversees them and can turn their hearts toward His will. When you reach the "never mind" hill, you don't get so upset about who is temporarily in charge of a temporary place. I pray for our country and our president whether or not I voted for the current president. God puts people in power and can turn even the president's heart to His will. Often the current leaders are just pawns in the greater story, like Pilate was.

In the moment of history we are going to look at, Pilate was the man in charge. In the time line of history, Pilate was a pawn in this story. I love that Pilate wrote that Jesus was the King of the Jews in Aramaic, Latin, and Greek. See, everyone could read it now. *Ha, you manipulative Pharisee hypocrites, I have the last word on this one.* I think by this time Pilate was beyond worn out by the wicked chief priest and slimy elders. Pilate did not want to crucify Jesus. He did so because of the chief priest and the angry, dangerous mob. Pilate went against what his wife had warned him not to do. Anyone who is married knows that was a really bad decision. Pilate listened to and was persuaded by the crowd. Like any mortal, he wanted to please the crowd he feared, even at the cost of his heart and his relationship with his wife. He caved. Human! So, by the time the chief priest started to whine about the sign I think Pilate felt like burned toast. He knew exactly what he was doing. He wrote the inscription in three different languages for the whole world to know for all eternity that **this is Jesus, King of the Jews on the cross.**

When we truly trust God, we can nevermind mean politics and pray for all our leaders. God is in charge!

"The Lord can control a king's mind as He controls a river; He can direct it as He pleases. You may believe you are doing right, but the Lord judges your reasons" (Proverbs 21:1–2 NCV).

REFLECTION

Do you believe God can control a leader's mind? Do you pray for your president and leaders? Write out a prayer for your leaders.

PRAYER

Lord, who we think is in charge, You have set in place. I trust You. I will pray for the leaders in charge and know You can turn their hearts toward You. Help me to pay no mind to mean politics and hateful agendas. Let me pray for all of those in governmental authority. You are the One who is truly in charge. Amen.

Brokenhearted but Full of Compassion

> It was now about noon, and darkness came over the whole land until three in the afternoon, for the sun stopped shining. And the curtain of the temple was torn in two.
> —Luke 23:44–45

On the "never mind" mountain, you truly understand what God, Jesus, and the Holy Spirit did for you. This is why I think the word *enough* was heard all through heaven and the earth. "Enough! This has got to stop because how things are going currently, it's just not working!" There is so much here in the foregoing verses. Jesus is hanging on a cross, exhausted, with a crown of thorns on His head, a bloodstained punctured face, ripped flesh grotesquely hanging, and nails in His arms and legs. Dirt, sweat, and a hint of perfume from Mary Magdalene surround this moment.

The most amazing thing about this moment is the ultimate surrender of hanging on a cross for the world's sin. I envision a host of angels being held back by Jesus's surrender! The very earth cries out! It turns dark. The earth shakes and the rocks split! Graves open and dead people walk around (Matthew 27:52). In Genesis 1:27 it says that we are made in the image of God. He loves us. He wants a real relationship with us. God knew that this had to happen to restore His relationship with us, and Jesus's surrendered prayer of "Not My will but Yours be done" made it happen. It got sealed with surrender and knowledge of the agony to come. Even so, I have to acknowledge that God had to be heartbroken. The very people whom He had called His chosen ones had just killed His Son. God had set up a really nice detailed system of how to worship Him and atone for one's sins, and provided clear, precise dos and don'ts.

Have you ever made a detailed request with exquisite details to follow for someone and they flat messed it up by adding to it, or manipulating it, or finding ways to work around it? I think we humans call these loopholes. Humans! God's detailed plan for His chosen ones got messed up and manipulated and was made unbearable for His people. The very ones told to share grace, mercy, and love had made it impossible to have a real relationship with God. It's like when Dad leaves some detailed rules and a description of what to do and what not to do and then, because we don't want to follow Dad's rules, everything goes awry. But here is the picture: Dad is home, and he's not happy. So that is why I have the liberty to say I think God was furious. It was His Son dying on the cross, as the sun stopped shining and the curtain of the temple was torn in two (Luke 23:45). God went to the temple and His huge hands ripped that thick curtain that separates us from Him in half from top to bottom. He turned the light off (it went dark over the whole land), and He changed the plan. "When all the people who had gathered to witness this sight saw what took place, they beat their breast and went away" (Luke 23:48). In modern terms, it is like a teenager having just thrown a wild doozy of a party and the police coming—then Dad showing up. Busted! There is a scattered group of partiers running for safety, and the others are just standing there in absolute terror, crying and saying they are sorry. Here is the good news for you and me from God: *Enough. Things around here are going to be different from now on. You messed up the old plan beyond repair. No longer will there be a curtain and a holy of holies where only the priest can come to Me once a year. That did not work. Enough of abuse and misplaced authority. From now on, if you want to talk to Me, come on in!*

Jesus opened the door. It's a new day, and we are doing things differently from now on. Do you hear that? We can walk into God's holy of holies and talk to Him! Do you see and understand what that cost and what that means? Death on a cross for our sins. The final atonement. Enough!

REFLECTION

List what God, Jesus, and the Holy Spirit did for you personally on that cross.

PRAYER

Lord, with trembling fear and respect, I walk into Your presence, covered in the sacrifice of Your Son on the cross. You are worthy of praise and honor, and all I can do is be in awe of Your love. Thank You, Lord. Amen.

Doors Open

> For the wages of sin is death, but the gift of God is eternal life in Christ Jesus our Lord.
> —Romans 6:23

You are thankful for the "never mind" mountain. The door to Christ is always open, and you discover the best way to spend your time is with Him. Hallelujah! We may now enter His gates alone, without an escort, and talk to God directly. Hallelujah!

At first, we walk in hesitantly, fearfully, and overwhelmed. Next, we walk in with awe and appreciation. Sometimes we just cry. We keep coming. It becomes more familiar. He is our friend. We enjoy His company. We find the door is never closed. Ever. We can skid in with our skateboard, we can kneel at His side, and we can even bring a snack. We lift our spouses, children, and friends into His holy of holies and find that we can bring our thoughts, prayers, sins, secrets, and hopes. We bring our doubts, fears, anger, and praise. The more we come, the more at home we become. We just like being there in His presence. It becomes a second home, and we long for it all the time. Eventually we get to walk in and stay. He welcomes us with a delicious supper, unlike anything we have ever experienced, and then shows us to our room. We realize we are finally home because of what was surrendered and done by the statement "Not My will but Yours be done." Thank You, Jesus, for propping the door wide open!

The door is open, and we can talk directly to God. We can read our Bible, worship, and pray. Nothing and no one will ever block this door again. We are free from manipulative religious bondage forever! Don't ever let anyone or anything block your door to Christ!

REFLECTION

The only thing that blocks us from fellowship with God is what we put in front of the door. Is there anything that is blocking you from hanging out with God?

PRAYER

Lord, I love being with You. I love resting in Your presence and hanging out. Thank You for allowing me to come into Your throne room and worship You. Amen.

No Matter What

> Then Nebuchadnezzar in furious rage commanded that Shadrach, Meshach, and Abednego be brought. So, they brought these men before the king. Nebuchadnezzar answered and said to them, "Is it true, O Shadrach, Meshach, and Abednego, that you do not serve my gods or worship the golden image that I have set up? Now if you are ready when you hear the sound of the horn, pipe, lyre, trigon, harp, bagpipe, and every kind of music, to fall down and worship the image that I have made, well and good. But if you do not worship, you shall immediately be cast into a burning fiery furnace. And who is the god who will deliver you out of my hands?" Shadrach, Meshach, and Abednego answered and said to the king, "O Nebuchadnezzar, we have no need to answer you in this matter. If this be so, our God whom we serve is able to deliver us from the burning fiery furnace, and He will deliver us out of your hand, O King. But if not, be it known to you, O King, that we will not serve your gods or worship the golden image that you have set up."
> —Daniel 3:13–18

To get to a "never mind" state of mind, you surrender. Surrender your plans and what you think you need. Say a prayer to God: "No matter if You answer this prayer or not, I will believe in You and trust You." Sometimes, it takes awhile to get to that place. Especially when you think that what you want and pray for is essential.

It was snowing on Easter. I was sitting in Rumple Presbyterian Church in Blowing Rock, North Carolina, in a tucked-away classroom with my sweet two-year-old. This is an old beautiful church made of stone and stained glass windows. It feels great in the summer, but the winter invites the cold inside. We had quietly left the service because my little one was squirming. The snow I was seeing come down on Easter Sunday was not welcome. Spring was what I needed in the weather and in my heart! February is a month I could skip. Just get me to March and April, when it is warmer, and then to wonderful warm summer. Don't go to the mountains for Easter! It is like going backward in weather time and going back to winter. This Sunday was unfortunately freezing cold. As I sat in that quiet room, I heard God gently saying to me in my heart, "It is going to be a little longer for you, too. You have got to be okay if your family has steady employment or not." I had become hyperfocused on my husband getting a job after two years of unemployment, MBA school, and odd jobs. I was worn out. I wasn't enjoying life as I should have; I was superfocused on income and a job because, as we all know, money helps to pay bills and buy food. It was here that my surrender happened. I thought about how Daniel's friends in the Bible were thrown into a fiery furnace for not worshipping the king and how Daniel was thrown into the lions' den for not worshipping and bowing down to a statue. What I love most about the stories in the book of Daniel is the surrender. Shadrach, Meshach, and Abednego did not care if they were saved or not. They would not bow down and worship a false god no matter what. They all knew that God could deliver them out of the awful situation, but they were not going to bow down and worship a false god no matter what:

When Daniel is thrown into the lions' den for not worshipping and praying to King Darius, he spends the night with the lions.

In both situations these men surrendered their lives, not knowing what would happen. God was more important than their right to live. They would not worship a false god no matter what.

My false god had become employment. I needed to surrender that goal, and I needed to know that God was going to take care of us no matter what, if we had a job or did not have a job. As the wet snow came down, my surrender took place. Yes, God can be trusted no matter what. I had a peace that passed all understanding and a knowing that if my personal winter was to last longer, it was going to be okay and God had it all in His hands.

REFLECTION

What is it that you think you need? Will you surrender that need to God no matter what, even if that need is never met?

PRAYER

Lord, You know that joy and peace is most often found in surrender. Lord, help me surrender to You no matter what. Amen.

Before, Beside, Behind—Time Traveler

> "I am the Alpha and the Omega" says the Lord God, "who was and is and is to come, the Almighty."
> —Revelation 1:8

> And if I go and prepare a place for you, I will come back and take you to be with Me so that you also may be where I am.
> —John 14:3 (NLT)

When you know, really know, that God is in charge, you receive a peace that passes all understanding. God owns time. You have a "never mind" perspective on life. Every second belongs to God. Prayer is amazing. God is amazing. Both prayer and God are not bound by time.

The idea of time travel fascinates me. It would be so fun to travel through time. As people, we are fascinated with this concept because of God. God is not limited by time boundaries. He is the Alpha and Omega, the beginning and the end. He goes before us, beside us, and behind us and is all around us. He can be in more than one place at a time. He hears all of us. He never runs out of resources. He is everywhere! We only slightly understand who God is and all His wonderful marvels. This is the God that created us, who knitted us together, who knows all, who created all. He is not bound by time, and He wants a relationship with us! Wow! God is the ultimate time traveler; He goes into our future to prepare a way. He goes into our past and heals us. At the same time, He is right here present with us now. He even gives us the gift of prayer time travel. He allows our prayers to be answered now and in the future! We can even go back in time and forgive others and cancel strongholds in the name of Jesus.

We can't time travel, but we know God, and He is not bound by time. We can prayer travel. Pray Psalm 139 (I suggest the NCV's rendition). God knows everything.

REFLECTION

Spend some time today prayer traveling!

PRAYER

Lord, You have examined me and know all about me. You know when I sit down and when I get up. You know my thoughts before I think them. You know where I go and where I lie down. You know everything I do. Lord, even before I say a word, You already know it. You are all around me—in front and in back—and have put Your hand on me. Your knowledge is amazing to me; it is more than I can understand. Where can I go to get away from Your Spirit? Where can I run from You? If I go up to the heavens, You are there. If I lie down in the grave, You are there. If I rise with the sun in the east and settle in the west beyond the sea, even there You would guide me. With Your right hand You would hold me. I could say, "The darkness will hide me. Let the light around me turn into night." But even the darkness is not dark to You. The night is as light as the day; darkness and light are the same to You. You made my whole being; You formed me in my mother's body. I praise You because You made me in an amazing and wonderful way. What You have done is wonderful. I know this very well. You saw my bones being formed as I took shape in my mother's body. When I was put together there, You saw my body as it was formed. All the days planned for me were written in Your book before I was one day old. God, Your thoughts are precious to me. There are so many! If I could count them, they would be more than all the grains of sand. When I wake up, I am still with You. Amen.

Fruit of the Spirit

> But the fruit of the Spirit is love, joy, peace, patience, kindness, goodness, faithfulness, gentleness, and self-control; against such things there is no law.
> —Galatians 5:22

There is lots of fruit at the "never mind" picnic. You eat one delicious fruit after another, in order, and it is a wondrous banquet. Have you ever thought about why the fruit of the Spirit are in the order they are presented in? There are so many miraculous wonders in the Bible ready to teach us how to live our best lives.

Without love, you cannot experience joy. Without joy, you have no peace. Without peace, you have no kindness. Without kindness, you have no faithfulness. Without gentleness, you have no self-control. It is like a nine-step program. First, you know that you are completely loved by God; then you can love. Your cup overflows into joy. Joy gives you a peace that passes all understanding. When you have God's peace, you can show patience. Patience and not being so self-focused allows you to be kind and show kindness. Kindness is expressed in faithfulness. Faithfulness is followed by beautiful gentleness. And all these combined give you steady, confident, godly self-control.

I think we should pray for the blessings of the fruit of the Spirit every day. We should live the fruit of the Spirit in order. We should receive the fruits in order. It is like a natural Holy Spirit wonder.

REFLECTION

Pray for the fruit of the Spirit for yourself and your family.

Write down what each fruit of the Spirit means to you and how you can share the fruit of the Spirit with others.

PRAYER

Lord, let me know that I am completely loved by You. Let me overflow in Your love to others. I receive Your joy. This joy gives me Your peace that passes all understanding. Bind patience on me. Let my patience be expressed in kindness. May kindness be displayed in faithfulness and gentleness. May all the fruit of the Spirit combined bring me self-control. Amen.

What's Right with You

> A person's wisdom yields patience; it is to one's glory to overlook an offense.
> —Proverbs 19:11

When you live a "never mind" lifestyle, you learn to overlook minor irritations and quirks and enjoy that which is wonderful. We all have quirks, wonderful, irritating quirks that make us who we are. Even if we don't always like our quirks or others' quirks, we can always find what we do love about ourselves and others. Most of the time we just need to look at the entire picture and then overlook what needs to be overlooked and love well. I would hate to miss out on a wonderful marriage, job, or friend just because of a few irritating quirks.

I just read the book *Born to Run* by Christopher McDougall. It is a wonderful book about running, health, and a hidden tribe. One of my favorite quotes from the book that describes some quirky super runner college students is, "There was never anything wrong with you that can't be fixed with what is right with you." Let that quote soak in. We all have our quirks, things we see as disadvantages or our odd ways of expressing ourselves.

If you concentrate on others' faults, then that is exactly what you will see. If you worship and stumble over your own lack, your supposed disadvantages, your hurts, your pains, and your terrible memories, then that is what you will see. You won't move on. You will stay jogging in place. Jogging in place is an awful way to live long term. If you can't get past the oddity, the hurt, the sickness, or the offense, then *you ain't going nowhere!* Running is wonderful. To run in the woods, on a beach, in the desert, or anywhere outside is a blessing. You need to move. You need to see the good in yourself that outshines what you consider your stumbling blocks. You need to see the good in others and forgive others. Just overlook and cover up offenses and hurts. Your pain, struggles, and quirks make you, you. It is part of the plan.

Don't define yourself or others by what is wrong, but by what is right. Nothing is all perfect or all bad. Life just doesn't work that way.

REFLECTION

Do you have a relationship that could go to a wonderful new level of love and caring if you would choose to overlook some quirks that are bothering you?

PRAYER

Lord, thank You for the total package. Let me concentrate on the good. Help my mind to be positive; forgive offenses—mine and others'; and celebrate the beauty and the wonder of people and You. Open the eyes of my heart so I can see myself as You see. Amen.

Overcomer

> You, dear children, are from God and have overcome them, because the One who is in you is greater than the one who is in the world.
> —1 John 4:4

We all have probably said "It is what it is" out of surrender. With God, "It is what it is" can be so incredibly beautiful. We surrendered, and then God gave us the strength to *overcome*. We might look or feel different from others now, but our very being radiates the love of God. We become like a "never mind" hero wearing a humble cape. Underdogs that come from behind and win inspire us all. I met a "never mind" tree recently. Let me tell you about my tree. I know God had the final say with this tree.

I took a picture of this unique tree. It had gotten knocked down on its side in a storm. Most of its roots appeared to be showing. But the little tree persevered. It just grew anyway. The tree went sideways for about ten feet, then anchored some more roots and began growing straight up. I am not sure how it managed to put a root system down halfway on its sideways parts to support the rapid growth upward, but it did so successfully. It was adorable and inspiring. It made for an outstanding place to sit. It was such a cute, humorous, happy tree that just went on with life after its tragedy of being knocked on its side. Similarly, God can do amazing things with a life surrendered to Him. He can take our biggest tragedies and heartbreaks and bring unique and wondrous beauty out of them. This tree was an inspiration and is my favorite tree out of the forest.

God makes us overcomers. Don't waste your heartbreak, tragedy and disappointments on self-focus and pity, instead become an overcomer and display the humble beauty of God in your story.

REFLECTION

Some of my favorite people are humble overcomers and love others well. They have nothing to prove or hide. How would your life change for the better if you could totally surrender to God and let him bring good out of your story?

How would your outlook be improved, and your life have more joy if you were to wear your humble "never mind" hero's cape every day?

PRAYER

Lord, I am a child of God. Because You are in me, I am an overcomer. The One in me is greater than the evil one who is in the world. Thank You, Lord. I am unique, and I am Yours. What was a tragedy has now become a unique miracle through You. A life surrendered to You is truly wonderful and better than anything I could have hoped for or imagined. Amen.

Take This Last Bite of Wisdom, Then You Tie Your Shoes and Get Back Out There!

> Therefore, since Christ suffered in His body, arm yourselves also with the same attitude, because he who has suffered in his body is done with sin. As a result, he does not live the rest of his earthly life for evil human desires, but rather for the will of God.
> —1 Peter 4:1–2

As you take one more bite of food at the "never mind" picnic, you reflect on how much God loves you. Life isn't always easy; it's hard most of the time. But this refines you and makes you better. As you look to the future and dwell on the past, you realize that life is full of suffering, and that's not all bad. The suffering refines you like gold in a crucible. You are better for it. Is it fun? Not at all, but it is part of being human and living on earth. You feel the presence of Jesus, and with a twinkle in your heart, you become wiser.

Jesus taught us how to get through life. He came and put on human skin, emotions, hormones—all that it is to be human—and showed us how to get through misunderstanding, betrayal, death, and sorrow. He taught us how to deal with fake religious people, how to love, how to forgive, how to laugh and joke, how to spend our time, and most importantly, how to pray and how to really live. He was vulnerable as a baby and as a man. He was obedient and honored His parents. He was kind by helping some folks out at a wedding who had run out of wine. He healed. He wept. He loved. He prayed. He confronted. He forgave. He showed us how to have friends and be a friend. He hurt down here. He asked not to suffer, but then He submitted to God's will instead of doing His own. On the cross, while He was dying, He continued to show us how to love and live. He asked God to forgive because humans didn't understand what they were doing. He took the world's sin upon Himself so we could be set free. He conquered death and rose again. He did this for us. For you. He loves you that much! When you really examine Christ, you see His scars, you feel His love, and finally you are willing to be hurt again. You are willing to love hard, take risks, and become all God created you to be.

You finally realize that being hurt and suffering is part of the adventure called life. You put on your brave Christ attitude that knows there will be suffering and persecution, and you get back into the real world.

REFLECTION

Jesus got messy. He lived. Are you willing to live a messy life too?

PRAYER

Lord, You showed us how to live. You showed us how to suffer; You showed us how to forgive; You showed us how to love. In this world there will be trouble (1 Peter 4), but You, God, taught me how to get through it. Cover me in You. Take over and let me live for You. Make me more like You. I don't want to leave this world having missed out on all the adventures because I didn't want to get hurt. Get me back in the game of life. Amen.

CONCLUSION OF SECTION X

Hurt, mourning, sadness, pain, and learning how to deal with what life brings us is part of the joy of being alive. We get to experience the highest of highs and the lowest of lows. The pain is the price we pay for living and loving, and it's so worth it.

In many ways we are able to pay no mind to the future pain because we know it is part of life and we don't want to miss out on wondrous living and loving. It's so worth it that we realize we are willing to be hurt again and again.

Section XI

HURT AGAIN

You love God and realize that life is just tough sometimes. You have let the hard things that have happened make you better. You want to share your story when appropriate and with those who need to hear it. You want to get back in the game of life, and you know that you must be willing to be hurt again because pain is part of this wonderful adventure called life.

On the following pages you will find devotions about willing to be hurt again.

How Long?

> Teach us to number our days, that we may gain a heart of wisdom.
> —Psalm 90:12

You are willing to take risks, to be hurt, and to care deeply for others. It's finally not all about you and your pain. You really love others. Life is short, and you have only so much time to love others. The days can be long, but the years are short.

Life happens quickly. We start our years off eager for the future and end our last days thinking about the past. "How long do we really have?" is the magic question.

"How much longer? Are we there yet?" We ask these questions over and over. When we are young, it is a whiny, "I am uncomfortable and really don't want to be in this situation anymore, especially in the car," kind of question. "Are we there yet? My legs are sweaty and sticking to the hot seat. My brother is pinching me, and my sister is way past the line that separates our spaces. I need to use the bathroom, and I am hungry. Are we there yet? How. Much. Longer?" As we become a little enlightened in our late teens and twenties, we often ask this question out of self-importance: "How long, Lord, will You wait to help me? Can't You just fix this situation and have the Second Coming? Can't You just take me out of this sin-stained world? I am tired and ready to go home!" After we have lived many moons and have experienced love, heartbreak, deaths, miracles, and tragedies, we ask this question out of deep concern, knowing we are all creeping toward our expiration dates. "How long? How much longer do we really have? There are many we love dearly who do not know You yet or who are in a state of rejecting You." Envision that there is a holy host of angels, warriors on horseback, being held back by the mighty arm of God. The horses are braying with steam coming out their noses, and the warriors on horseback have their arms raised with swords in their hands. The horses are rearing and are ready to charge! Justice will come.

Sometimes in our lives we like to see ourselves on horseback with God's army, swords in our hands, getting rid of all evil. Yes, we all want evil to go away. We want to get out of this sticky, sin-stained world. But right now, because of the love of Christ in our hearts, we slip off our high horses, sneak out of the line, and crawl to the other side so we can love others, pray for others, and watch God's mighty mercy prevail. How long? How long do we have to share God's love with others, to help the hurting, to give hope to the fallen, and to let others know that—*yes*—Jesus loves them? He has every single one of their hairs numbered. He cares about the significant details in the world and about their intimate thoughts. He cares about how their kids do on their tests, and He walks the cancer wards with their dying friends. He is before us, beside us, behind us. How long?

But do not forget this one thing, dear friends: "With the Lord a day is like a thousand years, and a thousand years is like a day. The Lord is not slow in keeping His promises, as some understand slowness. He is patient with you, not wanting anyone to perish, but everyone to come to repentance" (2 Peter 3:8–9).

Life goes quickly. How long do we really have?

REFLECTION

We all are creeping toward our expiration date. When you embrace the fact that you won't be on earth forever, you will find that being hurt doesn't matter so much anymore. How can you live more intentionally?

PRAYER

Father, we know that You are in control of time. You know the past, the present, and the future. Lord, don't let me waste time or waste opportunities to share Your love and kindness with others. Help me to care more about others than about my pain, my hurts, and my agenda. Help me to love well and be willing to risk and possibly be hurt. It's about You, not me. Help me not to be so anxious about sharing Your love that I turn others away by forcing my agenda on them and being unattractive. God, thank You that You are patient and for the fact that You want no one to perish but for everyone to come to repentance. I lift up my loved ones and those who don't know You yet. Remove anything that is blocking them from knowing how much You love them. Lord, I pray the verse from 2 Corinthians 10:5: Lord, demolish arguments and every pretension that sets itself up against the knowledge of You, and, Lord, take captive every thought to make it obedient to Christ. All lies of the enemy are canceled in Jesus's name. Thank You, God, that nothing is impossible with You. Amen!

Jump Back In

> Not only so, but we also glory in our sufferings, because we know that suffering produces perseverance; perseverance, character; and character, hope.
> —Romans 5:3–4

The best part of being willing to be hurt again is that you live! You have fun again. You aren't afraid to take risks and maybe really be hurt again. Weebles were a very popular toy when I was a kid. You could knock them down again and again and they would just wobble back to a standing position again. Be a Weeble. Get back up again and again. Jump back in. Live life to the fullest!

Watching my kids play contact sports was gut wrenching for me. They would get knocked down, and every mama cell in me would want to get out of the stands, run to them, and make sure they were okay. Mostly, they would get back up. They had a few concussions and broken bones on the occasions when they didn't get back up. The insane thing is that they would heal and then go back and play that same sport again. Sports are great because they teach you to get back in the game even after you've had the poo knocked out of you.

Life sometimes knocks the poo out of us. Do you remember the AllState commercial awhile ago that showed a scene of kids playing in the ocean amid the rain, and the announcer said, "Man-eating sharks live in every ocean, but we still swim. Lightning strikes somewhere in the world, but we still play in the rain. So many things can happen." Great commercial! Life is unfortunate sometimes, and love hurts sometimes. Accidents happen, death takes our loved ones, and disaster strikes, but also miracles happen, along with laughter, love, and enjoyment. Life can be great! We shouldn't give up and hide or make goofy promises to ourselves that we will protect ourselves so we will never, ever be hurt badly again. It's the scars that make us interesting and tell our stories. It's the wrinkles and gray hairs that show our wisdom and character. It's not being afraid to swim again after shark bites that makes life enjoyable again.

We each get only one life. Don't bubble wrap yourself if you have had a rough, tough time. Wake up, shake it off, and go tackle life. You've got this!

REFLECTION

What kind of risk do you need to take to live a full life?

PRAYER

God, thank You that our sufferings produce perseverance; perseverance produces character; and character produces hope.

Lord, let our suffering, pain, and sadness be for only a small season. Don't let us waste our pain and fail to learn from it. Father, help us quickly learn and move on to perseverance, kindness, and empathy for others with a great, holy, godly character that reflects Your love and peace to all. Let us not only receive Your hope but also share Your hope with others. Help us cuddle in Your arms and then frolic in Your wonderful world. We love You, God! Amen.

Relationships

> For God so loved the world that He gave His one and only Son, that whoever believes in Him shall not perish but have eternal life.
> —John 3:16

When you are willing to be hurt again and love through the hard times, you just need to rest in the messiness and realize Jesus understands and gets it.

Have you ever needed to be friends and communicate with someone because he or she was an integral part of your life? I'm not talking about a bestie from second grade! This is someone you should be in a relationship with: a daughter, son, daughter-in-law, spouse, or parent. For whatever reason, the person doesn't answer your texts or phone calls; he or she even blocks you. The person won't respond to letters. He or she cancels meetings and ignores you. Even if the conversation would be a difficult one, it would be better for the person to let you know what you did wrong or how to make the relationship work. At the very least, couldn't the person just tell you how you offended him or her so you could fix the problem? Days go by. Weeks go by. And the next thing you know, it's been years. You ache! You hurt! There is such sadness and a hole in your life where that person should be. You desperately reach out. You forgive unconditionally. You would do anything to restore the relationship or even *have* a relationship. It is an important relationship to you. You pray that the relationship becomes full of love, laughter, and significant memories. Fellowship. You always had pictured your relationships full of fellowship. You lay flat on your face, begging God for restoration. And God whispers to you in your heart. He understands. He so, so, so understands. You just want fellowship with that person. Your heart aches. He gets it. He has been there. He has loved and loved and loved too, only to be ignored, hurt, and defamed. My dear one, He understands. He too wants only fellowship, love, and a relationship with each one of His daughters and sons. He understands your pain and rejection, so much so that He was willing to send His Son to earth, to be born to a teenage mother in a dirty stable, in a sin-heavy world, to restore His relationship with you. He gets it, my precious one. He gets it.

God understands and experiences messy, hard, heartbreaking relationships, too. He gets it.

REFLECTION

Life can be very hard. Comfort yourself with the knowledge that God faces the ultimate rejection from His creation willingly and repeatedly. He hates not having a relationship with us. He gets it. His sacrifice for us is an absolutely insane kind of love: Jesus died on the cross to restore His relationship with us, and even so, He still gives us a choice to accept or reject that gift. Ask God for that kind of supernatural love, wisdom and perspective. Write down how this changes you and comforts you.

PRAYER

Father, You know what it is like to hurt and feel the overwhelming pain of rejection. I ask You for healing in this situation. I ask that You cancel rejection and misunderstandings in my life. Let there be no bitter roots or unforgiveness found in me. I ask that those who have hurt me and those I have hurt take comfort in Your arms. Nothing is impossible for You. I cling to You. Bring Your hope, healing, and love. Help me to love well, to be willing to be hurt again, and to see people the way You see them. Amen.

Ask

> Yours, Lord, is the greatness and the power and the glory and the majesty and the splendor, for everything in the heavens and on earth belongs to You. Yours, Lord, is the kingdom; You are exalted as head over all.
> —1 Chronicles 29:11

Ask, because if you are willing to be hurt again, then you need to display some faith! Don't ask for what you know God can do. Ask for what *only* God can do. If you truly believe that God is our good heavenly Father, then you are not shy about asking Him for anything. An earthly father wants to bless His kids. Your heavenly Father wants to bless you, too; He wants you to ask.

My son had a horrific accident two years ago. He fell off a rope swing that left his arm with a severed nerve that didn't quite heal and some fingers that he can't feel yet. He just had another surgery to try to get all of it to heal and work properly. The nerve is in a tight ball on both ends where it was repaired. That is what is giving him so much pain. The doctors scraped away the scar tissue but might have to do another surgery for it to completely heal. I was praying with my son for complete healing, and then I thought, *Wait, I'd better not pray that. What if God doesn't answer it?* But then I thought, *What if He does? What kind of faith am I showing my son if I only pray for things I know God can do? That is a sad, shallow, fake faith.*

When my sweet niece was five, her mom asked her what she wanted for Christmas, and she said a candy cane. My sister laughed as she was telling me about it and said it was so funny to her because her daughter had asked for so little when she wanted to give her so much more. God thinks a similar thing about us all the time. None of us want a candy cane faith! We don't have to hold back when we talk to God. He owns the entire universe. He is the Creator of heaven and earth. Say 1 Chronicles 29:11 out loud.

So, let's ask and ask big. Let's pray those kinds of prayers that only God can answer. Let's dance in the arms of God and have His vision instead of ours. Let's tell God our dreams and then defer, saying, "Not my will but God's!" We don't always see the big picture. And God has not answered all my prayers! One of the best songs is by Garth Brooks, "Unanswered Prayers."

It is beautiful, and its lyrics are so true. Garth, you are right, sometimes God's greatest gifts are unanswered prayers. However, as I am sure Garth knows, sometimes God's greatest gifts are answers to those prayers that are so bold that the only explanation is God. Let's be the sort of Christ followers who ask big and then trust either way.

REFLECTION

Start praying prayers that only God can answer. Write them out.

PRAYER

Lord, You are the Healer. You are the owner of heaven and earth. Everything belongs to You. You always know my hair count. You want to bless us and prosper us and are more interested in who we are than in what we have. I trust You. I know You know my heart's desires. You know my inner thoughts. I will ask You for miracles and trust that, like a good Father, You know what is best. You are good. Amen.

The Bench

> Yet to all who did receive Him, to those who believed in His name, He gave the right to become children of God.
> —John 1:12

We would all rather be playing and working, especially when we are planning on playing or working. No one plans to be fired, furloughed, or left to sit on the miserable sidelines! Sometimes you've got to work through the disappointment while you are hurting. It's part of being willing to be hurt again. It's life.

If you have kids who play sports, or if you play sports, you have probably sat on the bench some, *not playing*. It's no fun sitting on the bench. Sometimes you are on the bench of life because of a job loss, a move, advised bed rest, or an accident. You want to be in the game of life, but for whatever reason, you are still sitting on the bench. Bench time can tell you lots about who you really are and about what and who defines you. If you use bench time wisely, you can learn more about who you are when you sit on the bench during sports or life than about who you are when in the game. It is definitely more fun to be playing and even more fun to be the best player. But sometimes to get there, you have to endure some bench time. On the bench you learn to celebrate others or wish your team was losing since you aren't playing. On the bench you learn to work harder so you won't be on the bench anymore. Or you just stop trying and maybe even quit. On the bench you learn either humility or bitterness. On the bench you learn forgiveness, especially if it is bench time for political reasons—and many times it is just that. You are good enough to play. On the bench, you decide: Do you want to keep doing this and work to get off the bench, or will your time be better used elsewhere? Bench time can be more important in the development of a person than playtime. It's when you dig deep and know that you are not defined by how good you are on the field, but by who you are on the bench. Do you know yourself? Do you know who created you? God loves you and wants you to know you are His masterpiece!

Life can be very frustrating. We want to be working and to be a part of the game of life. *We are good enough to play and work!* When we are on the bench, it gives us time to reconnect to God. Our worth comes from being blessed children of God. This is who we are.

REFLECTION

How can you use bench time to become a better you?

PRAYER

Lord, I am a child of God. This defines me. This is who I am. May every cell in my body radiate Your love, and may I reflect Your glory and Your will. Help me to get through hurts and pain with Your perspective on the situation. Amen.

Healthy Fear

> One of the criminals who hung there hurled insults at Him: "Aren't You the Messiah? Save Yourself and us!" But the other criminal rebuked him. "Don't you fear God," he said, "since you are under the same sentence? We are punished justly, for we are getting what our deeds deserve. But this man has done nothing wrong." Then he said, "Jesus, remember me when You come into Your kingdom." Jesus answered him, "Truly I tell you, today you will be with Me in paradise."
> —Luke 23:39–43

If you are willing to be hurt again, you need a healthy fear of God. When I was talking with a friend about praying for her daughter, she asked that I pray for the fear of God in her life. With a smile, she explained that when you pray for the fear of God, God hears you. Understanding the fear of God can make a life-changing difference in our lives.

Three men. Two guilty, one innocent. One is angry, defiant, and guilty. One knows He is guilty but fears God. One is holy, innocent with the world's guilt upon him and with the ability to forgive. Don't you fear God? Do you fear God? According to Google, fear is an unpleasant, often powerful emotion caused by anticipation or awareness of danger; profound reverence and awe, especially toward God; and reason for alarm. *Danger.* God is dangerous and all-powerful and owns everything in heaven and on earth. I grew up in the generation where people really respected their fathers. I love my father. I can high five him, and now that I am an adult, we are friends. But I also have so much respect for him. I fear him in a good way. I don't want him to see me mess up or to disappoint him, but I know if I do, he will forgive me. *Fear* is a word we don't like. It sounds negative, but it can also be healthy. You don't play hopscotch on the highway because that would be dumb, and you could get killed. You have a healthy fear of playing hopscotch on the highway. The highway is good; it can get you from one place to another quickly. You don't play with sharp knives or let your toddler play with sharp knives. Sharp knives are great when used to cut food. They are also dangerous if you chop your finger instead of the vegetable. You fear and respect the knife and learn sometimes the hard way how sharp it can be. The knife isn't bad, but it can be dangerous. You need a healthy fear of it. When you come into the presence of God, you should have a healthy fear full of holy honor, awe, praise, respect, and thankfulness.

"The fear of the Lord is the beginning of wisdom, and knowledge of the Holy One is understanding" (Proverbs 9:10).

If you want to powerfully pray for yourself, someone you love, and your nation, then pray that for the fear of God in your life, your loved one's life, or the life of your nation. I have seen miracles happen when I pray that. We all desperately need the fear of God in our lives. Three men. Two guilty. One innocent. The fear of God made all the difference.

"Today you will be with Me in paradise" (Luke 23:43).

REFLECTION

How can having the fear of God in your life protect you from harm?

PRAYER

Lord, may the fear of God be in my life, in my family's life, and in our nation. May we love, respect, and honor You with holy awe. Lord, teach us to truly live, and help us to be willing to risk and be hurt again. Most of all, Lord, bathe us in the fear of God, which brings us wisdom and knowledge of the Holy One. May Your Holy Spirit give us protection and wisdom. Amen.

Love Always Protects

> It [love] always protects.
> —1 Corinthians 13:7

If you are willing to be hurt again, sometimes you love someone so much that you are willing not to be liked for a while. True love protects and speaks up for those you love. The love and safety of that person trumps all hesitation to confront the person or get help for him or her.

The 1970s and '80s were a great time to grow up. It was easy back then to have a good, pure outdoor childhood. *Play* was the primary focus. Playing kick the can, swimming, being outdoors, building forts, swinging on rope swings, playing hopscotch, riding bikes, fishing, canoeing, playing pretend, building sandcastles, swinging, playing tag, playing pickup games, putting on skits, catching crawfish—we did all this and more. Idyllic childhood memories. When the bell rang, we went home for dinner. Other than that, we were outside playing. I loved it. When I look back at some things we did, I laughingly wonder if maybe natural selection was still in vogue during my childhood. We did some insane "don't ever share with Mom" stuff. We all did. However, my sister would always tell on me when I ate wild mushrooms. Why I did this, I am not sure. I do like mushrooms to this day, and I have always been a practical person who tries to save time so I can get the most out of every moment, so maybe I just was hungry and wanted a quick snack and didn't want to bother going inside! I didn't want to miss anything.

I remember exactly where I was standing the last time my big sister told on me *again* for eating mushrooms. The mushrooms were growing in our yard. That was before serious pesticides prevented these delicious snacks from growing in the yard. Out would come the confession that "Yes, I ate the mushrooms in the yard," and in would go the ipecac syrup. Then I would spend the afternoon throwing up. I think this happened three times, my sister's being a tattletale having caused me to spend the afternoon hugging the toilet. That is all it took, just three times, and I no longer ate mushrooms in the yard. I have, however, found out how to collect edible mushrooms in the forest. It is a great springtime activity and is safe. The point is, I am glad my sister told on me now. I could have died or been really messed up mentally as some mushrooms are poisonous.

Sometimes you need to tell someone, that is, be a tattletale, and get the help your loved one needs. It could be a matter of life or death. In our politically correct society, sometimes we feel that we can't confront. Real love speaks up, calls people out, and gets you help even if the one you are helping gets mad at you and has his or her feelings hurt by your help. Sometimes it is a life-or-death matter. You have to be a tattletale! Love always protects.

REFLECTION

Is there someone in your life that you love enough to tell the truth to and get help for? Could it be a life-or-death situation if you don't get the person the help he or she needs?

PRAYER

Lord, help me love others enough to protect them and speak the truth in love. Let me be teachable so that others feel comfortable helping me. Lord, be in charge. Amen.

Sea Glass

> And those who belong to Christ Jesus have crucified the flesh with its passions and desires.
> —Galatians 5:24

Good comes out of brokenness. That is what makes us beautiful. You know this deep in your core, and it doesn't scare you anymore to get hurt. What happens to you makes you, you. Hard times can make you like refined gold or sea glass, depending on how you look at it.

Topsail Island in North Carolina has some rough waves. Just like rough waves, rough times can toss you around and wear you out. As I walked on this beach, I could see others picking up things on the beach. All I could see was broken shells at first. Then I noticed shiny and smooth round pebbles that were fun to touch. Sea glass. Beautiful. These broken pieces of glass were being collected as treasures on the beach for the ones who found it. I reflected on my journey these past several years. I felt like a bottle tossed out into the sea. I felt discarded like trash, broken, crushed, and pounded by the waves of sorrow, anger, disappointment, selfishness, doubt, fear, and manipulation. I was broken, mad, hurt, desperate, and sad. I slowly surrendered. I stopped wanting my way and my agenda. I finally let God take over. As I picked up a piece of sea glass, I felt such joy. The sea glass and I have lots in common. I am the sea glass in so many ways. I like myself so much better now. I am beautiful in the brokenness, and I am so incredibly thankful for the journey. My surrender makes the hard sharpness of the broken pieces of my life smooth and worthy of being treasured. The broken parts of our lives will become smooth again and again as we get tossed in the waves of life.

Life is so much more than being broken. It is about being made into what we were meant to be: beautiful treasure!

REFLECTION

Many times in life, we stay in a place where we are broken but not broke. When we give up and give all our brokenness to God, we become broke, and in that brokenness, we become treasure. Are you broken or broke right now?

PRAYER

Lord, continue to crucify the flesh in me with its passions and desires. I live through You. I am Your treasure. You are my life. You are my treasure. I am Yours. In Jesus's name. Amen.

Rough People

> But I say to you, love your enemies, bless those who curse you, do good to those who hate you, and pray for those who spitefully use you and persecute you.
> —Matthew 5:44 (NKJV)

When you finally can say, "Change me, Lord! Change me!," you are ready to start the next chapter and really live again. "Change me" requests are often made when you are in a hard situation. You have loved, forgiven, and given it your all. You are around some difficult folks. Things aren't changing, so your only option is to ask God to change you.

We all know sandpaper people. They are just not pleasant to be around. Negative, mean, cruel, manipulative, emotional imbeciles, gossips, and no-filter kinds of folks come across all our paths. It is a real pain when we deal with them daily. It is just plain rough: sandpaper rough.

Every time you get near these people, you get scratched. But do you know what sandpaper does? It smooths the rough spots. It gets rid of the blemishes. It spiffs you up and makes you better: smoother, kinder, more pleasant to be around, and worth more. It fine-tunes you. How, you wonder? You learn not to be offended, to love unconditionally, to pray for your enemies, and to bless those who persecute you. You learn to depend more on God, to empathize, to have a soft answer when provoked, and to show the love of Christ. As rough as it can be to be around sandpaper people, they really can be a blessing to your well-being. You get the benefit of loving others, praying for others, blessing others, and needing nothing in return. That, my dear, is a wonderful skill to have.

We all want smooth skin, smooth personalities, and smooth lives, so sandpaper people really are one of the blessings of a life well lived.

REFLECTION

A change in perspective and a change in yourself helps you see your life differently. Write down how the sandpaper people and sandpaper situations in your life help you become a better you.

PRAYER

Lord, show me how to love my enemies, help me bless those who curse me, let me do good to those who hate me, and give me the prayers to pray for those who spitefully use me and persecute me. Change me, Lord. Change me. Amen.

CONCLUSION OF SECTION XI

As we end the devotions about being willing to be hurt again, I hope joy dances in your soul and you realize that being hurt is the price we pay for living. The more we live, the more we open ourselves up to the wonders of the world. We can handle pain and love well. We don't want to miss out, and we are determined to live life to the fullest!

Section XII

LIVE LIFE

Through love, hardness, and messiness, I see the miracles of God! I am not afraid to be hurt. I want to live, really live, with the wind in my gray hair, with scars on my body, and with laughter in my heart and grace bombs going off everywhere.

On the following pages you will find devotions about living your best life.

Hunter or the Hunted?

> Do you not know that in a race all the runners run, but only one gets the prize? Run in such a way as to get the prize.
> —1 Corinthians 9:24

When you can look back and thank God for the storms in your life or be wise enough to know in the storm to hang on and enjoy the ride, you are living! Hold on! Often, what you need in order to get where you should be is a little external motivation. Like the winds of a hurricane or a lion at your back, you need an extra push.

Sometimes I think we think we are going as fast as we can and doing the best we can. We are trying as hard as we can. We think we are giving it our all. Then suddenly something intense, tragic, or frightening happens, and it is as if we become the hunted. We can forgive where we thought previously something was unforgivable; we can love in a way that now allows us to pray for our enemies; we can give more than we ever thought possible; and we can laugh through hardship and find joy in the pain. We really are making it and even thriving amid the times in our lives when we are lonely, forsaken, and mistreated. We are being refined as gold in a crucible. This extra pressure, fear, and intensity helps us realize that we had a lot more in us than we realized. We are not just running to get the prize but are running for our lives. We go so much faster and farther than we could have without this intensity and pain. When we reach the finish line, we are very thankful for the pressure, the pain, and the intensity that helped us get there. It is as if a lion chased us, and because of that we ran and performed so much better than we ever thought possible. I truly believe that God places the lions in our lives to be a blessing and to get us to where we should be. So, we run in a way to get the prize, and God helps us get there with His lions at our back, letting us know that we really can run, live, and do this thing called life in a much better, more beautiful way.

Let's be thankful for the lions and storms that come our way that bring us to places we never would have gotten to without them.

REFLECTION

What storms or lions at your back have taken you to places you never thought you would go or be able to handle?

PRAYER

Lord, so many times we just want comfort and ease, but what we really need is "hustle" and refinement. Thank You for providing the motivation to keep us going. Thank You for the times in life when You refine us. Thank You for always caring more about who we are than about what we have to go through. You want us to be everything we were created to be. You are good and worthy of praise. Amen.

Backpack

> Apples of gold in a setting of silver is a matter spoken at its proper time.
> —Proverbs 25:11 (LEB)

When you delight in life, you delight in the simple things. You see miracles all around you. You treasure people, and you are very thankful for what God has provided for you.

There are some relationships and things in life that are more special than others. Most of the time it is because we make those people or things more important. We focus on those people and things.

You have only so much time on earth, so choose wisely, and when you choose, treasure those you choose. That makes them special.

When my son Andrew entered kindergarten, my husband and I did a little experiment about saving money. We selected an expensive, higher-quality backpack for our five-year-old to see if it would last through to his senior year. We washed the backpack at least two times a year and sprayed it with Lysol frequently. Andrew is very sentimental and loves the fact that he has had the same backpack all these years. It has shared his school journey with him. If it could talk, what stories it would tell! And the savings added up: 13 years of school × a new $35 backpack each year = $455. Sometimes it pays to buy quality. Quality time, quality people, and quality things make life better and also make it easier to maintain a healthy lifestyle. Waiting for the right moment and the right place to talk about a matter is essential. It's all about timing and treasuring what we have. We can get too busy and become unproductive and worn out with sports, music lessons, church, overwork, too much stuff, volunteering, and so forth. Andrew has concentrated on a few things and does them well. Life is short. Choose quality people, quality things, and quality time with God.

Proverbs 25:11 reminds us to be intentional. Treasure the good things of God, and don't waste your resources. There is a beautiful silver bowl displaying my apples that reminds me of this verse and its instruction to live an intentional simple life. I am very proud of Andrew for keeping the same backpack from kindergarten through to his senior year. His backpack is his apple of gold in a silver setting. It is important to treasure what you believe is important to you.

REFLECTION

What steps do you need to take to be more intentional and treasure those in your life?

PRAYER

Lord, help me treasure what I have.

Let me treasure and invest well in my loved ones' lives.

Lord, make me intentional in loving and appreciating people and what You have given me to take care of. Prevent me from squandering time, resources, and opportunities. With the people You bring into my life, let me take time to love them, invest in them, and encourage them. Let me appreciate and take good care of my material possessions. All belong to You, Lord. Let me live fully in the moment and enjoy your blessings. Let the people in my life feel loved by me and by You. Help me, Lord, to honor and treasure others. "Apples of gold in a setting of silver" is how I want others to feel treasured and loved by me. Hear my prayer, Lord. Amen.

Generous

> Kindness to the poor is a loan to the Lord, and He will repay the lender.
> —Proverbs 19:17 (BSB)

When you are truly living, you live as if all of heaven and earth belongs to God. Your stuff doesn't own you. You are a giver. You bless others.

My husband, Daniel, is a generous man. Sometimes when he gives, it hurts a little. My mother-in-law loved to tell a story about my husband when he was little. When Daniel was five, they were visiting a family in need, and Daniel noticed the little boy about his age didn't have any shoes. He took his shoes that his mom had just bought him and gave them to the little boy. What his wise mom did was to have Daniel wear his old shoes that were a bit snug until she had budgeted for a new pair of shoes—about three months. Daniel felt the pain and the joy of that instantaneous decision to give his brand-new shoes to a little boy in need. It didn't dampen his giving personality whatsoever. Still today, if he sees a need, he takes care of it. Sometimes it hurts, and sometimes it is easy.

If you can learn to have a giving heart in times of plenty and in times of want alike, then you will know the true joy of giving. What you have is not really yours anyway. All of it is God's. He just lets you enjoy His blessings for a while.

"Cast your bread upon the waters, for after many days you will find it again" (Ecclesiastes 11:1 ESV).

Give, bless others, and be generous. God will take care of you. God will take care of those to whom you give generously, and He will take care of you. Sing this song with me (by Civilla D. Martin, 1904).

God Will Take Care of You

Be not dismayed whate'er betide.
God will take care of you.
Beneath His wings of love abide.
God will take care of you.

God will take care of you
Through every day, o'er all the way; He will take care of you.
God will take care of you.
Through days of toil when heart doth fail, God will take care of you.
When dangers fierce your path assail, God will take care of you.
All you may need, He will provide; God will take care of you.
Nothing you ask will be denied; God will take care of you.
No matter what may be the test,
God will take care of you.
Lean, weary one, upon His breast.
God will take care of you.

REFLECTION

Since all of heaven and earth belongs to God and you know God will take care of you, doesn't that free you up to be more generous?

PRAYER

Lord, give me a giving heart even when it hurts. Teach me to be content in plenty and in want. I trust You. You are the owner; I am the borrower. It all belongs to You. Amen.

Snort Laughter

A merry heart does good, like medicine, but a broken spirit dries the bones.
—Proverbs 17:22 (KJV)

When you are enjoying life and really living, you laugh! You laugh until your sides hurt! You take time out from life and laugh! Laughter is healing. There is nothing better than a merry laugh with those you love.

There are a handful of people whom I can truly snort laugh with. I'm talking about the type of laughter that starts with a snort and, after a long time and many funny stories later, ends with your stomach being sore. My favorite "snort laughter" friend is my sister. She knows things about me, and I know things about her, that are locked in the vault, never coming out. We share our childhood memories; we share parents; we share our experiences raising kids; and we share the good, the bad, and the ugly. The best part: she will call me on things I do wrong. We overtalk everything: beat it to death, then resurrect it and talk about it again.

Somehow my husband's phone and my phone are linked, and he sees who I call and how long I talk. He finds it amusing. "Today you talked to your sister fifteen times." Yeah, buddy. You, my husband, should be so thankful. I live in a house full of men. Men can't handle how many words I must get out each day. They would go bonkers if I were to unload my word quota on them each day. They should all be singing the Hallelujah chorus and thank God I have a sister who will talk to me. When she and I get together, we laugh, we pray, we tell funny stories, and we share secrets. It's good for my soul.

Find snort laughter in your life and people who can lock things in the vault. You can only truly laugh a genuine snort laugh with those who truly know you and love you anyway. Laughter is the best!

REFLECTION

It takes only one good friend to snort-laugh with. How can you be a better friend to others?

Do you need to be more vulnerable? forgiving? honest? loosened up? not always win? just have fun?

PRAYER

Lord, thank You so much for friends. Thank You for the healing power of laughter. Thank You that we are created in Your image and that You want us to laugh and be happy. Thank You for knowing all about us. Lord, thank You for giving us merry hearts and healing us with laughter. Amen.

Expired Party

> I give them eternal life, and they shall never perish; no one will snatch them out of My hand. My Father, who has given them to Me, is greater than all; no one can snatch them out of My Father's hand. I and the Father are one.
> —John 10:28–30

We all have an expiration date. God knows our expiration date like a bride knows her wedding date. He's getting ready for us! He's planning our party! We are going to party like we have never partied before. We just graduated!

My dad had brain surgery this past summer. Before the surgery, I told him he was in a win-win situation. If he were to die, he would get to be with Jesus. If the surgery were to go great and work, he would get to enjoy some more years down here with us. I am not afraid of death at all, just maybe of how I go.

If we really understood that when we die, we get to be with God, then we would have a party instead of a funeral. We could even have a destination funeral like people have destination weddings. How fun would that be?! No matter what, let's get dressed up in party gear, drink some wine, remember all the good times, and celebrate our loved ones. Have a band, make toasts, and do some dancing! Being with our heavenly Father is something to look forward to! We just graduated!

Yes, I will miss those still on earth when I die, and y'all will for sure miss me, but I know that we will all eventually get to spend eternity together! Jesus is the way and the truth and the life. In John 14:6, Jesus says, "I am the way and the truth and the life. No one comes to the Father except through Me."

It is very easy: confess your sins and ask Jesus into your heart. That is something to celebrate. Let's party!

"Where, O death, is your victory? Where, O death, is your sting? The sting of death is sin, and the power of sin is the law. But thanks be to God! He gives us the victory through our Lord Jesus Christ" (1 Corinthians 15:55–57).

Eternity together forever! No sting here. Just a party. Turn up the praise music!

REFLECTION

When we get to heaven, it's going to be a party! Why not have the party on earth too?

Do you want a funeral or a party when you depart?

If you could plan a destination funeral, where would you want your loved ones to visit?

PRAYER

Lord, we don't know all the details of how heaven will work. But we do know that we get to be in eternity together forever when we ask Jesus into our hearts. We will get to worship You and praise You and proclaim with the heavenly host of angles: "Holy, Holy, Holy are you, Lord God Almighty, who was, and is, and is to come" (Revelation 4:8). Thank You, God. Amen.

Well-Liked

> When they had crossed, Elijah said to Elisha, "Tell me, what can I do for you before I am taken from you?"
> "Let me inherit a double portion of your spirit," Elisha replied.
> —2 Kings 2:9

There are some great people on earth, people who you want to be like. Seek them out. Hear their stories and learn from them. Living a good life involves learning from others.

As I get older and experience having adult children and hanging around others with adult children, I hear either, "I keep my mouth shut and don't offer my opinion unless asked" or "I wish I had kept my mouth shut." The greatest compliment a mom can get is for her kids' spouses to have many conversations about how great she is and how lucky the spouses are that she is their mother-in-law. My husband, brother-in-law, and sister-in-law adore my mom. We all do. There are so many jokes about mothers-in-law. But my mom is no joke. She is kind and keeps her mouth shut and doesn't get into others' business. Ever. Her rule is that she doesn't give her opinion unless I directly ask her. She prays fiercely for her kids, their spouses, her grandkids, and her great-grandkids. She is funny and forgives easily. She does not demand or manipulate. She loves the Lord.

Have you ever heard of a generational blessing? It is a blessing that one person passes down to the next generation, who passes it down to the next generation and so on. My husband just got his Ancestry.com DNA report, and it let him know of illnesses he could be more prone to getting or not get because of his ancestors' genes. Spiritual blessings and wisdom can be passed down, too.

I really, really hope that I get my mother's humor, love for God, and ability to pray for others, and mostly that I inherit from her the ability to remain quiet and not stick my nose where it doesn't belong. I'll ask her to pray for that for me. She will. In fact, I am going to be bold and ask like Elisha asked Elijah in the Bible. I am going to ask for a double portion. Lord knows I need it. I want to be the person in the group who says, "I keep my mouth shut and only give my opinion when asked."

REFLECTION

We all want to be well-liked and be a blessing to others. Ask God for wisdom and protection in your relationships. Obey Him. How can you be well-liked?

What generational blessing do you want?

List generational blessing that you want to leave to others.

PRAYER

Lord, I ask for the blessing of inheriting kindness, not interfering in people's business, not being manipulative, and having great faith, a prayer life, and a great relationship with my children, my children's spouses, and my grandchildren. I ask that You bless my family line with each person knowing You, loving You, and hearing at the end of our lives, "Well done, good and faithful servant." Amen.

Sifting

> As iron sharpens iron, a friend sharpens a friend.
> —Proverbs 27:17

If you are really out there living, you are often going to find yourself in new places, without family or friends to rely on for support. You took some risks, and now loneliness is your new best friend. Be patient with yourself and with the process of finding a friend.

It takes a lot of work to find a friend, especially if you are a little shy. It is like panning for gold in a stream. You start with a lot of material in your pan, then you keep sifting and throwing stuff out—rocks, pebbles, dirt. You keep putting water in your pan and gently sift. On and on and on it goes. You can't do this too fast or you will lose the good stuff. Similarly, you can't rush a friendship. Especially in a new place. There is going to be a lot to choose from. The big rocks might look right at first. They represent the popular standout people. Most of the time, the big rocks are just big and take up too much space. The pebbles can be good, but maybe not good for you. Dirt? Just stay away. It just gets you in trouble—and it never pays to follow the crowd. You should be careful when you see gold. Some of it is fool's gold. People who look like they may be nice and a good influence end up being fools and stabbing you in the back. Be careful; keep sifting. Be wise and discerning. Finding a genuine friend is hard. It might take several times to get some genuine gold or precious stones. Don't give up. Once you find some golden friends, hold on. Be good to them and let them be good to you.

It takes only a few authentic people to make life great. Keep panning. They are out there!

REFLECTION

What do you need to do to have good friends and be a good friend?

PRAYER

Lord, thank You for providing friends in Your perfect timing. Amen.

"Live Well" Lifestyle

> If I speak in the tongues of men and of angels, but have not love, I am a noisy gong or a clanging cymbal. And if I have prophetic powers, and understand all mysteries and all knowledge, and if I have all faith, so as to remove mountains, but have not love, I am nothing. If I give away all I have, and if I deliver up my body to be burned, but have not love, I gain nothing.
> —1 Corinthians 13:1–3 (ESV)

Go on the mission trip, say yes, come back, and be a missionary all year long to everyone. If you go on a mission trip and don't change your lifestyle the other fifty-one weeks of the year, then I am not sure it is worth your time.

I love mission trips, and this is why: it makes me humble, grateful, and thankful. It strips me of my privileged upbringing and privileged life. I could have been born anywhere to anyone. If I have clean water and a nice bed to sleep in, then I am privileged and quite rich. A mission trip is one small week that can transform a life, especially for those serving, who often receive more than those being served. It changes your attitude and your heart. It reminds me how to live and how to love others the other fifty-one weeks of the year.

We will all have to account for every lost moment and every opportunity of every day. Were we kind to the new kid at school? Did we help someone not feel so lonely in the cafeteria or at work? Did we include those we know who would have loved to be included? Did we stick up for the bullied? Were we Jesus to others?

We need to live a lifestyle every moment where we love others like Jesus would.

REFLECTION

How do you need to change so you can be a missionary every day of your life?

PRAYER

Lord, let me love others the way I would on a mission trip every single day. Let me be the hands and feet of Christ to my family, friends, and neighbors. Lord, let my whole life be a mission to love others in Jesus's name. Amen.

Water

> No eye has seen, no ear has heard, no mind has conceived what God has prepared for those who love Him.
> —1 Corinthians 2:9

Live well. Celebrate, dance, go to the deep end, and plunge into the goodness of the Trinity.

I barely understand the love that Jesus, God, and the Holy Spirit have for me. The Trinity can be confusing to us because we are bound by earthly ways. Water helps me understand the Trinity better. I love water. I love to drink water, I love to swim in water, and love the fact that it keeps all of life alive. Water helps me understand the Father, Son, and Holy Ghost: the Trinity. How can They be all the same and yet so different? Then I think of water and its purity. Ice. Liquid. Steam. All the same, yet so different. Without water, I wouldn't even be able to stay alive. Without God, I am just a dehydrated, confused mess! When I pray, I often pray to God, Jesus, and the Holy Spirit. It's a party. I think we as humans barely understand the amazing, miraculous way God, Jesus, and the Holy Spirit love us and work together.

Because I thirst, I will never not be thirsty. I will always need water like I always need God, Jesus, and the Holy Spirit.

REFLECTION

What do God, Jesus, and the Holy Spirit mean to you personally?

PRAYER

God, Jesus, and the Holy Spirit, let us be in the category of those who love You. Help us know the Trinity. Let our cups overflow with Your living water. May we splash, dance, and share the joy of the Lord with others! Amen.

I'm Hungry

> And while they still did not believe it because of joy and amazement, He asked them, "Do you have anything here to eat?"
> —Luke 24:41

If you want to live well, then learn to be vulnerable and eat with your bare hands like Jesus did! We all need people in our lives with whom we can be vulnerable, hungry, and honest, with whom we can eat with our hands while food dribbles down our chins. This is the good stuff that makes life worth living! Jesus showed us how to have friends and how to love.

Jesus shows up from death hungry. He's with His best friends, being real. His last supper was literally the Last Supper, and it was a long time ago, before He died. Jesus is with his inner circle, His buddies. His question: "Do you have anything to eat?" I'll translate that into modern southern language: "Yep, I just hung on the cross, died, went to hell and back, and revealed Myself to all of y'all, and now what I really want to know is, what do you have to eat? I'm starving!" I don't know about you, but there is just a small group of people I can say such a thing to. "Yep, all of that was tough, good, bad, and messy, and I am laughing and crying at the same time. What I really need right now is something to drink and eat, so what's in the refrigerator?"

While they were still talking about this, Jesus Himself stood among them and said to them, "Peace be with you." They were startled and frightened, thinking they saw a ghost. He said to them, "Why are you troubled, and why do doubts rise in your minds? Look at My hands and My feet. It is I Myself! Touch Me and see: a ghost does not have flesh and bones, as you see I have." When He said this, He showed them His hands and His feet. And while they still did not believe it because of joy and amazement, He asked them, "Do you have anything here to eat?" They gave Him a piece of broiled fish, and He took it and ate it in their presence. (Luke 24:36–43)

Jesus wants us to have peace. Don't you want that for yourself and your loved ones? Peace. We are often frightened, startled, and scared. So, Jesus just addresses the issue. *What's the problem? Look at My hands and feet. Touch them. Dude, ghosts don't have flesh and bones.* This next part of the verse is so human: "What do you have to eat?"

Joy and amazement. Too good to be true. Laughter through the tears. Overwhelming emotion and a hungry human stomach. I can just imagine a piece of broiled fish being handed to Him. No plate, no napkin, just a piece of fish in the hungry scarred hand of Jesus. The kind of eating took place then that you do with those you love. A little grease dripping down your hand and chin. You're just hungry and you eat what's in front of you: *yes, with your bloodstained, scarred hands*. That is when you know you are with your people, the ones you are vulnerable and real with. You can show them the ugly, the good, and the great; that which is hard; and the sin and evil; and be hurt by them, hurt them, and know that you will all still love one another, forgive one another, and be great friends. You can laugh at each other's weirdness and peculiarities. These are the friends to whom you give grace bombs, from whom you receive grace bombs, and with whom you share laughter, tears, and hardship—the ones to whom you can say, "Where is the dark chocolate and ice cream? Let's talk."

You know what is so cool about this? It was Jesus at His best: human, relatable, vulnerable, and yes, hungry. He is with His best friends. They are friends who betrayed Him, but He loves them anyway. That is the sort of relationship He wants with us. I bet when the story about this was recorded, the disciples chuckled and smiled, and they all agreed, "Yes, the part about Jesus asking what we had to eat is included. That was just who Jesus was. Holy. Human. Forgiving. Hungry."

REFLECTION

When you read your Bible and study just how human Jesus was, it is very comforting. Do you allow others and yourself to just be hungry (i.e., be human)? Why or why not?

List ways that you can be more vulnerable in your relationships.

PRAYER

Lord, You dwelt among us. You had Your feelings hurt; You forgave; You were in pain and were thirsty and hungry. Because of the grace that You showed, You taught us how to have and be friends. You taught us to love, forgive, and be real. Thank You. Amen.

This Little Light of Mine

> You are the light of the world. A town built on a hill cannot be hidden. Neither do people light a lamp and put it under a bowl. Instead, they put it on its stand, and it gives light to everyone in the house. In the same way, let your light shine before others, that they may see your good deeds and glorify your Father in heaven.
> —Matthew 5:14–16

People who are living the good life shine with the love of Jesus! Remember the Sunday school song "This Little Light of Mine" (a children's song written by Harry Dixon Loes)? Letting the light of Christ shine in your life is important. It is important to be a kind, attractive Christian and be so much like Christ that you bring others to Him because of how well you love. Telling others about Christ is a delicate matter. Make your life shine so beautifully that you barely have to open your mouth.

Before cell phone flashlights, a Big Daddy flashlight could be a powerful force. It could light the way, help you in the dark, or annoy you when someone flashed one in your eyes and practically blinded you. As a kid, you had the power if you had the flashlight, and that power could be either kind or mean, depending on how you used it. Sharing your faith can be the same way; it can light the way or make someone feel blind, judged, and annoyed. A candle can soothe and change the entire atmosphere of a home. It can bring hope. Candles on a cake represent joy and celebration. A fire can either warm up the home or burn down the house depending on what kind of fire it is.

God wants us to be a light to others. Be a kind light. Be gentle. Show the way. Be attractive. Give grace, mercy, and forgiveness. Don't put your bright light right in people's faces and therefore blind them. Doing so makes them feel less than and judged. Know that just like a birthday candle, your time is short. Bring joy. Warm up others like a cozy, inviting fire. Be a blessing. Don't get out of control, take over, and cause the house to burn down just because you want something so badly that you fail to honor boundaries.

Let God, the true light, shine through you. Be beautiful.

REFLECTION

Write down ways you can shine the beautiful light of Jesus toward the people in your life.

PRAYER

Lord, make my soul beautiful and attractive to others. Let people see You in me. Stop me from forcing my agenda on others. You are in charge. Use me to shine an attractive, beautiful, Christlike love to others. Lord, You burn down the lies of the enemy that separate us from You. That's your job, not mine. Thank You that through Christ, His light can shine in me. Thank You, God. Amen.

Notecards

For this reason, I kneel before the Father, from whom every family in heaven and on earth derives its name. I pray that out of His glorious riches He may strengthen you with power through His Spirit in your inner being, so that Christ may dwell in your hearts through faith. And I pray that you, being rooted and established in love, may have power, together with all the Lord's holy people, to grasp how wide and long and high and deep is the love of Christ, and to know this love that surpasses knowledge—that you may be filled to the measure of all the fullness of God. Now to Him who is able to do immeasurably more than all we ask or imagine, according to His power that is at work within us, to Him be glory in the church and in Christ Jesus throughout all generations, for ever and ever! Amen.
—Ephesians 3:14–21

Part of living well is being intentional. The sentence in Christian groups "I'll pray for you" can slip and be forgotten, even it's said with good intentions. A good friend in college taught me how to intentionally pray for others.

If I say I am going to pray for you, I will. Thanks to a beautiful woman named Sandy who mentored me in college, I learned to take prayer and the memorizing of Bible verses seriously. She taught me to write verses and people's prayer requests on notecards and to flip through them, praying and worshipping that way. I have about thirty notecards that I flip through every morning. Written on these are things to pray for others and myself, verses to memorize, and prods to remind myself to be thankful. I update the cards frequently with different verses and different prayer requests. This simple practice helps me be intentional and keeps me grounded.

I am very thankful for prayer for myself and others. It's important to be intentional about prayer.

REFLECTION

We have all been guilty of saying "I'll pray for you" and then forgetting. Either pray for that person right then or there or write yourself a reminder so you won't forget.

PRAYER

Lord, help me pray for others. God, teach me to memorize scripture and pray Your Word. Lord, bring others into my life whom I can pray with. Lord, You always do immeasurably more than I can ask or imagine. Thank You. Amen.

Sing, Shout, and Dance

> Therefore, I tell you, her many sins have been forgiven—as her great love has shown. But whoever has been forgiven little loves little.
> —Luke 7:47

If you want to really live, then share your story and be inspired by others' stories. Party when someone is healed or finds the Lord.

In my Bible study, there was a woman in my group who had been healed after a devastating car accident that had left her body in shambles. She was so full of this wonderful miracle that she glowed when she talked about it. That same year, I experienced a life-changing situation, and she was the first person I thought to call. She walked me through it and helped me heal.

Being around people who have just been saved or healed is one of those delightful gifts we get to experience on earth, especially those who are older and know that they have been rescued and received a God-ordained miracle. If you have ever really sinned and been separated from God, or if you have been sick and then healed, you have something to celebrate. I mean, put on your dancing shoes, sing, praise, and tell anyone who will listen! "Amazing Grace" is one of my favorite hymns. It was written by a previous slave trader who found Jesus, which changed his whole life: his career, his outlook, and his purpose. Being around people who have experienced these kinds of beautiful undeserved miracles is like seeing joy bubbles pop all over the place. The person knows he or she doesn't deserve it, and that is why he or she is so passionate about having been set free. You can't keep such a person quiet. I love it.

No one deserves grace or earns it. If I could fly a plane, I would scribble a great big "Thank You" in the sky to my sweet friend who walked me through a dark time and into the light. It is important to celebrate and tell others about your miracles and healing. You might just be someone's next appointment with amazing grace.

REFLECTION

Do you know in your core that you don't deserve amazing grace? How does this undeserved grace help you love others better?

Do you need to share your story so you can help and bless others?

PRAYER

Lord, thank You that I have been forgiven much. All of us have. I celebrate You and worship You. Use me to help others. Let me rejoice in others' miracles! Amen.

Hey, Can You Play Today?

> And He said, "Truly I tell you, unless you change and become like little children, you will never enter the kingdom of heaven."
> —Matthew 18:3

Playing is living. It's fun and good for your soul. Play is very important. Do you remember the phone calls or the knocks on the door when you were little when a friend interrupted a rather mundane day to see if you could play? The joy! *Someone wants to play with me! I am important enough that someone wants to take time and play with me!* If you are a parent, the way to show children your love is to play with them. It makes them feel valued. You show your children they are more important than work, the cell phone, friends, and the never-ending schedule. We get to play! Yippee!

My brother Paul has a childlike heart. He is like an otter in that he sees play as being of the utmost importance. It's hard to keep up with him; one needs to train just to be up for a visit. I love that for business meetings he always meets for a milkshake. It's sweet and endearing. He is comfortable in his own skin, and he really is a golden retriever at heart. Play is important! He needs to run a camp. He is constantly starting pickup games of anything he can think of: tag, basketball, soccer, Frisbee, manhunt, or anything fun! He is creative, kind, and funny, and it's hard not to smile when you are around him.

God tells us to become like little children or else we won't enter heaven. Picture yourself as a little kid jumping into the pool with your heavenly Father standing right there to catch you. Be like a child. Jump! Jump, with complete and utter trust, into the mighty arms of God! Develop a child's heart.

Frolic and enjoy yourself, spend time with God, and spend time with those whom you want to feel valued. When my brother Paul walks into heaven, I picture him barefoot and chewing gum, with an ice-cream sandwich in one hand and a crayfish in his other hand. If there are pearly gates, he will probably hang on one of them and swing back and forth in pure joy.

REFLECTION

How can you make more time to play?

Write down something fun you can do today, this week and this weekend. Follow through.

PRAYER

Lord, teach me to become like a little child and frolic in Your wonderful ways and in Your world. Give me a childlike faith that knows You've got me no matter what. I trust You. Amen.

I'm Good

> A good man brings good things out of the good stored up in his heart, and an evil man brings evil things out of the evil stored up in his heart. For the mouth speaks what the heart is full of.
> —Luke 6:45

Life dials should always be set to "I'm good" because God is good. How we set our attitude and outlook dial truly determines the direction of our lives.

The last time I heard my friend Carolyn use her favorite expression "I'm good" was when she was upside down with her feet in the air and her arms sprawled out, yet still able to display a thumbs-up sign. She had rocked too far back in her comfy chair and taken quite a funny tumble. Carolyn has set her life dial on "I'm good." She decided a long time ago she was going to be good. Since I've known her, which has been for a very long time, I've been able to tell if she is struggling. When I ask her how she is doing, and if she says, "I'm goooooood," that means things are hard and she is choosing to look for the good and be good. Remember the T-shirts "Life Is Good"? Those are good T-shirts, but the slogan is not always true. Life can be tough, messy, tragic, and good. Carolyn could wear a T-shirt that says "I'm good" because she decided a long time ago to be good. You know why? She loves the Lord, trusts the Lord, and lives for the Lord, and deep down, even through heartache, tragedy, and death, she knows ultimately that she is good because she belongs to the one who is good: God!

Let's all set our life dials to "I'm good" because we know the One that is good!

REFLECTION

Where is your life dial set, on good, mad, bad, hurt, disappointed? If you were to set your life dial on good, how would that change your life?

PRAYER

Lord, let me praise You and thank You every day for who You are. Let me see the good in life and know that I am good because You are good. You've got me. I can rest in You. Peace that passes all understanding is from You. Amen.

Getting Mileage out of Life

> Mary treasured up all these things and pondered them in her heart.
> —Luke 2:19

To truly be living is when you live with both muck on your shoe and joy in your heart. You choose to remember the good and are able to grow from the hard parts of life. O look forward to God's promises, treasure them when you experience them, and rock the experience like a baby in your memory.

Mary treasured all the good things of God in her heart. It is as if Mary rocked the knowledge of God, the Words of God, and her own experiences as she would rock an infant. She cuddled the memory of the angel that first visited her, the miracle of conceiving Jesus, the long ride to Bethlehem, the smells of the stable, the first glance at Jesus, the coldness of the desert night, the angels, the rough-looking shepherds, and the huge star. She treasured the miracles amid the mundane. She dwelled on the majesty of God in a dirty stable. Because Mary treasured all these things in her heart and pondered them, she didn't forget them. The love, grace, and miracles swirled inside Mary's heart during Jesus's childhood, reminding her of who He was in His adulthood. Tragically, Mary remembered the miracles of His birth while she watched Him hang on the cross. It blew across her memory and her understanding. It shaped who she was and how she reacted.

We need to journal, ponder our journey with God, and tell others about it. Let's share our stories, good, bad, and tragic, and our failure to understand, with others. When miracles happen amid the mundane, we need to rock these memories, treasure them, and ponder the greatness of God.

My sweet grandma used to love when I visited. How do I know? She would tell me. She would want to know the date way before it was to happen so she could look forward to it. She would make me feel very special when I was there, and then she would tell me she would relive the visit in her mind. And then she would relive the visit with me on the phone. She used to say, "I'll get a lot of mileage out of this." Why should we be any different? Ponder, look forward to, enjoy, and then remember. We have only one life. So, let's get a lot of mileage out of it.

REFLECTION

What can you do to get more mileage out of life?

PRAYER

Lord, help us to treasure up all the good, including Your love, our memories, and Your saving grace. Let us ponder Your amazing ways and Your love in our hearts, even in the difficulties, even when there is muck on our shoes. Amen.

Farewell

We are made in the image of God. He wants us to be happy and take delight in Him and who He made us to be. I don't apologize for asking for a funeral/destination party when I go to meet my Lord. I have enjoyed life down here on earth and plan on living hard to the end. If I were a drinker, I would drink and toast to mostly everything, even the hard stuff, because I have grown tremendously from it. So, in my heart and with my attitude, I will do just that. It is really a short life after all. We all have an expiration date, and none of us are getting out of here alive. So, we should enjoy, celebrate, learn from the pain, and let God contend for us. A toast to me, a toast to God who made me, a toast to you, and a toast to love, forgiveness, and joy! May we all swim and play in God's mirth! I challenge you to declare a "year of you" and then a "lifetime of you." God wants you to be happy and be the best you. It's not a dress rehearsal down here, so you might as well make it the best life possible!

> O holy Father, Jesus, and Holy Spirit, You are God, and I am not. All of heaven and earth belongs to You. Even the trees clap their hands to praise and worship You. Your mercy, grace, and forgiveness are never-ending. Your death on the cross set me free to come to You wherever and however. You are uncontainable, all-powerful, worthy of being feared, dangerous, tender, and intimate. Nothing is impossible for You. You can redeem any hurt, mistake, or situation. I don't deserve any of Your kindness, forgiveness, mercy, favor, or grace, but You give it to me anyway. All of life gets its breath from You. At the end, every knee shall bow, and every tongue confess that You are God, our Lord and Savior. You are my best friend. You have always cared about our relationship. You pursue me.

> We are all made in the image of God. Nothing can separate us from the love of God unless we let it. You take all the dumbness away from us and give us the mind of Christ so that nothing does separate us from You. You are worthy of praise. I thank

You for loving me, for my family, and for all of creation. I thank You for your undeserved mercy, forgiveness, favor, grace, and wisdom that You give me and to all those whom You love, which is all of creation. I thank You for the tender relationship and for caring about all of me, all of us. You are good and worthy of praise. Help me bring You glory. Amen.

In Conclusion

Life can be hard—messy hard. I hope that by reading *There Is Joy in My Heart and Muck on My Shoe* you can conclude that life is hard but also wonderful. You don't want to miss out on that which is wonderful just because life is not perfect. The idea for writing *There Is Joy in My Heart and Muck on My Shoe* started with a question from a friend who was hurting and wondering if she would ever be okay. The really important questions for all of us is to wrestle with are "What kind of person do I want to be? How do I want to handle hard things?"

My Long Answer to a Question:

"How do I recover and how long will it take for me to be okay again?" This was the question that the beautiful, intelligent twenty-year-old woman asked me at lunch. She didn't share what had happened in detail, just that a previous boyfriend had left some serious scars. From my experience—and I say this carefully, *my experience*—I have found that one goes through many stages on the road to healing. It is hard, uphill, and bumpy with many U-turns, falls, mistakes, and needed rest stops.

Prepare

If you can learn from your own experiences, others' experiences, the Bible, and wisdom from God, then you can be a little more prepared when you step in something awful.

Shock

You've just hit the bottom of a deep, deep valley. You stepped off a cliff, or you were pushed off a cliff you didn't see. You are bloody and hurt. *What just happened? This can't be real. I will wake up from this nightmare and be relieved it was just a bad dream. Please, please, please, God, take this away. Fix this.*

Help me! You are doubled over in pain, despair, and grief and you realize, *It happened, and this is now my reality.* All you can see around you are sheer rocks with no handholds and no way out. You are in so deep that you can barely talk or communicate with others. Your only hope is the wish that this had not happened.

Share

You look around and you see some ropes. Some look safe and some do not. You see a warning sign on the rope that reads: "Please remember that you never, ever have to share your story with others." You can keep things private or public; it is up to you, depending on how you want it to affect your family and those who love you. A death is shared. Some things don't have to be shared. Once it becomes public, though, you can't take it back. It is like once you spill the milk, you can't put it back in the jug. It is everywhere and spreads and drips. Really, really pray about whom to share this with and if those you are considering talking to can be trusted. Prayer can become gossip. In big capital letters, a sign says, Be wise. You look at the rope for a long time and you see a little inchworm on the rope, which is saying over and over again in a high voice that hurts your ears, "In my opinion, err on the side of not sharing with others." You look at both ropes and you know you must decide. Then you see graffiti on the wall in bright red paint that reads: "Most of all, you decide when and if you share with others. Give yourself time." You sigh with relief. You see a rope labeled "Grace" and grab on.

Grace

There are tiny butterflies all over the rope of grace. They are singing to you a sweet melody: "Grace for yourself. Lots of it. Lather it on and let it soak in deep. Take a long run-out-of-hot-water shower of grace." You do so, and it feels great. In the shower of grace, you give yourself permission: you do not have to do the things you normally schedule and probably shouldn't. You can cancel, take sick days, and tell others no without explanation. Avoid certain people, situations, and triggers. Allow yourself to have time. You have a gaping wound, and you need stitches and healing. You might need to see a counselor and to let your work know that you are going through a hard time. You do not have to give any details at all. Cry. Mourn. Be sad. If you still have to function, as most of us do, just get through it and fake it. Put on a nice outfit and fake a smile. Then go home and fall apart in private. Protect yourself and your family.

Mourn

Right outside the curtain of the shower of grace is a place called Mourn. Sit down and allow yourself to mourn. You can choose your spot—in the desert, by a stream, or in a lonely cabin. Wail. Cry. The Old Testament Jewish custom was to hire mourners and wail. Literally or figuratively rip your clothes and put on sackcloth. However your personal sackcloth works and ripping your clothes works, allow yourself to be sad and cry. Express your disappointment and anger to God. Tell Him what you really think. He can handle it. It is healing. Cry yourself out. Cry the type of crying that gives you a headache, then do it all again the next day. Mourn for what you and your family have lost. Get it all out. Don't be brave. Allow God to put a blanket around you and sit down beside you and let you cry. Don't rush. Stay here as long as you need to, because the next step is hard.

Angry

This is a platform, and it is okay. Stand on it. Get your anger out. Yell at God. Scream at the top of your lungs. Express your disappointment, frustration, and anger to God. Tell Him what you really think again and again. Remember, He can handle it, and He will handle the problem for you. It is healing to get it all out. He is after your fellowship after all. A long way past your platform of angriness, there is a small warning sign handwritten on a post in the ground. The ground is dirty here. There is no avoiding the mess if you go this way. You are going to get black sticky dirt on you. The sign is yellow, and the words are scrawled in red: "Please don't turn to food and addictive substances during this stage." Behind the sign, there is loud music and smoke, and you can see huge tempting platters of sorrow and bitterness. Don't eat from these. Behind the platters are huge metal containers of toxic, addictive temptations. They are labeled, "Drink and smoke this if you hate yourself, God, and life. You will feel better!" On the containers it is written: "Drown yourself and your sorrows forever." There is a vast crowd of young people who look to be having fun who are calling out to you to come and join them. The older crowd just sit around with tired eyes and don't even look up or look your way. You look around and realize there are many signs in this place: Exercise. Swim. Run. Get counseling. Fellowship. Church. Friends. Be still. They all have ads and promote their healing power in shiny letters. Some are pretty. Some are not.

Sweat out your anger. Lift weights. Walk. Be alone. In this place, you need to give yourself some alone time each day just to scream and be angry. Don't do this in front of young kids, please. Swimming is great because you can scream under water and nobody can hear you. You get to decide. It is up to you. But eventually, and hopefully, you are going to tire of being angry. Then you'll discover that way out beyond all the signs and glitter and flashing lights is a bed covered in soft beautiful cotton with pillows that call out to you. You think about how nice it would be to rest.

Rest

Being angry is exhausting. It takes a lot of energy to be angry, and after a while you just need to take a long rest. It is up to you if you want to rest and then go back and revisit the stages of grace, mourning, and being angry. You can go in and out of these spots for as long as you need. But after a while you really do tire of it all and you know you are healing, so you might be ready to forgive. This is when you are probably going to run into some trash.

Dump

Trash is gross, and it is nasty to hold onto things that should be thrown away and forgotten. I want you to imagine what your living space would look like if you never took out your trash. At first, it wouldn't be so bad. Just some fresh trash in the trash can. Next, you'll have trash bags next to your trash can. Maybe you'll have some pizza boxes on the counter. Then come some rinsed-out milk bottles, some wrappers, some containers, and maybe even a couple of dirty diapers on your counter. Spoiled food and leftovers stink and begin to pile up. Add a couple more weeks and you have mold growing. Give it a month and you now start to throw up if you walk near your once clean living space. You stink. Your spot on earth stinks, and people are avoiding you. You need to take your trash out, and you need to bathe. This is no longer a grace shower but a scrub brush shower. Use some serious soap and spray some Lysol.

If you can't take baby steps toward forgiveness, you are going to smell awful and people will not want to be around you. You might have to move to the dump, where other dump dwellers live. Misery loves company. Do you really want to live in a dump? I don't think so. But many people do. They aren't nice and aren't nice to be around. Hurting people tend to hurt people. Many take their lives here. If you look carefully, though, you will see there is a tiny exit door labeled "Forgiveness."

Forgiveness

Forgiveness: It is not for the weak at heart. Many see it and laugh and prefer to stay angry. These people like to show off their hurts and injustices as if they are medals they have earned. They like the dump. It feels good to be angry. They feel justified. Vengeance! If you go through this door of forgiveness, you will find it is straight uphill, but at the top there is an exquisite view. You walk through this door and you bump straight into the cross. You look at it hard and see bloodstains. You see sticky notes and graffiti all over it. You read it, and it looks familiar to you. You see the things you have done on that cross, and you see the things done to you on that cross. You just sit at the cross and realize that you and your sins nailed Jesus there. Then you see the things that others have done to you are also nailed to the cross.

You can stay there in guilt, condemnation, and anger, or you can look a little farther and run into the bloodstained arms of Jesus and get a great big long-needed hug. He can comfort you and stroke your hair and let you know what your hair count is today. He can wipe away your tears, and you can just rest in His arms. After a long while, you can look into His eyes, where all you see is love, a love that you have never experienced before. It makes you cry, but these are good tears: tears of joy, release, and peace. Your heart overflows. You never want to leave. You just stay here in His presence. You stay for a long, long time, but after a while you realize this love and peace is too great not to share. So you gradually climb your hill again, only to bump straight into the person and situation that hurt you. You want to run back into the arms of Jesus, but then you look up and realize it is His arm reaching out to you to help you climb up this hill. In His eyes and in His voice, you see and hear that you can't go any higher if you can't forgive. He reminds you, "I forgave you while you were sinning." You can even look back and see the cross in the distance and see your sins on it. Your soul screams, "I want to be forgiven!" As you reach for Jesus's hand, you say to the person who hurt you, "I forgive you because He forgave me."

We don't deserve it. I don't deserve to be forgiven, and you don't deserve to be forgiven. As you push up on this foothold and grab onto God's hand, you see a beautiful view, but then you look down at where you came from and you see those terrible memories, which causes you to slip. You fall hard and hit your face on the ground. When you look up, Jesus is there with some bandages, a sandwich, some water, and a harness. He wants to belay you up the mountain. You smile, get some rest and much-needed food, and start up the steep hill of forgiveness again. As you climb higher, you feel lighter. You praise God and thank Him for what is good, for what you have, and mostly for His love. You grab hold of the rock that shouts, "Pray for your enemy," and next you swing up to the rock that sings, "Bless those who persecute you." You are holding onto a ledge that sings as you grab it. "Mighty is the Lord, and worthy to be praised." You might slip and have to start over again and again. Each time you fall, Jesus is there to pick you up again. His eyes always radiate His love for you.

After a while you realize that this is a journey and it's okay to fall and slip and climb again and again. You are getting good at being humble, scraped up, bandaged up, and most of all forgiven. You are also getting good at forgiving others. Sometimes Jesus climbs beside you, and sometimes He pulls you up. It is the relationship with Him that you enjoy. After a very long time you reach a pinnacle, and it is labeled "Never mind." You are confused, and you look at Jesus thinking, *This is not what I expected at all.* He looks at you with a twinkle in His eye and asks you to sit down for a picnic.

Never Mind

The "never mind" picnic is so much better than you could have imagined, and it tastes much better than anything you've ever tasted before. It is food that you've never tasted before with mixtures of ingredients that you never thought would have worked together. It is bitter, sweet, spicy, and smooth. It makes you laugh. As you chew, you realize that it does not matter what others think. It only matters what God thinks about you. He loves you. You look into Jesus's eyes and you laugh again. It is just between you and Him. The picnic is cozy and warm, and the food is delicious. You take another bite, and you discover that what you're eating has toasted nuts in it. You smile and think about how people can be nutty and dumb and can say cruel things. You taste a bit of honey and know that you will be okay when people say mean and dumb things. And Jesus reminds you of what He cried out on the cross: "Father, forgive them, for they know not what they do." As you swallow, you taste the power of going ahead and forgiving others before they even hurt you. It tastes delicious. It is a release. You relax. The warm sun on your face feels wonderful. You feel happy. You take a sip of joy, and smile. You laugh until your sides hurt, and then you pop some chocolate in your mouth and just enjoy eating it. You stay here a long time. Then you see Jesus looking in the distance. He is smiling. You see the mountain called Willing to Be Hurt Again, and with a smile from His heart, He hands you a backpack with some water and delicious food and pats you on the shoulder. And you hike.

Hurt Again

Willing to be hurt again is a mountain surrounded by air that is fresh and smells so great that you feel alive like you have never felt before. There is a delicious sweet breeze. You breathe in deeply, and a pleasant warm sort of air fills your lungs. You can taste a delicious flavor like the beginning of spring and hope. There is a kind breeze that wraps around you and makes you feel loved. There are beautiful-smelling flowers, exotic birds, and mossy knobs. The sky is a soft blue. The birds are all singing the most beautiful melody you have ever heard, and even the wind whispers, "You are loved." It feels somewhat familiar but all new at the same time. You look around and you see puppies chasing their tails and butterflies teasing the puppies. Everywhere you look, you see love. A cute little mouse eating a chunk of cheese winks at you. You see only one other person on that hill, and when you walk closer, you see that she is smelling a beautiful white rose and smiling. In fact, you now realize the sweet smell that you first smelled is from the rose garden that she is tending to. The rose garden goes on for as far as you can see. Roses on trellises, roses on the ground. It goes on and on. All the roses are an ivory white. It looks like snow, and when the wind blows, the petals dance for joy as if they are singing a sacred song. The woman in the garden sees you and waves. She is old, a beautiful old. Her wrinkles smile. Her gray hair glows. She needs a cane to balance herself, but she does so gracefully. She is beautiful and wise. Everything falls still. An air of respect surrounds her. Her eyes have a confidence and beauty in them. She sits down on a bench in the rose garden and laughs. She hands you a rose.

You take a whiff of that sweet-smelling rose and you laugh and cry at the same time. You look down and see that your hand is bleeding from the thorns on the stem, but you realize that it is okay. It is worth it. The old woman looks at you with wisdom and with a knowing in her dancing eyes. Your new friend puts a bandage on your hand and has a smile on her face that only you two share. You feel the greatest peace. It is a peace that passes understanding. You have no idea how long you have been here. Time doesn't seem to exist here. Way out in the distance, bathed in the most beautiful sunset you can imagine—red, pinks, and a little soft green—are the barely visible valleys of shock, mourning, and anger, and you think that you can make out something that seems to be a dump that is covered in beautiful red light from the sunset, so it doesn't look like a dump at all. You think about the climb of forgiveness and the picnic of "never mind," and you smile as you realize that this is life. And you want to live it. You want to live it well. You sling your backpack onto your shoulders and run. Your being is back and is willing to live, love, and be hurt again.

Live Life

You live; you laugh; you forgive; you have scars; you have glorious memories. You're wise; you learn from the difficulty; and you lift your hands in the air and your gray hair flaps in the wind. It's been a noble life; it's been real. You have taken every last sip you can of life, and you go out with a belly flop and a giggle.